ADULT LITERACY

ADULT LITERACY

Issues for
Policy and Practice

Hal Beder

KRIEGER PUBLISHING COMPANY
MALABAR, FLORIDA
1991

Original Edition 1991

Printed and Published by
KRIEGER PUBLISHING COMPANY
KRIEGER DRIVE
MALABAR, FLORIDA 32950

Library of Congress Cataloging-in-Publication Data

Beder, Hal.
    Adult literacy: issues for policy and practice/
Hal Beder.—Original ed.
        p. cm.
    Includes bibliographical references and index.
    ISBN 0–89464–476–9 (alk.   paper)
    1. Literacy programs—Iowa—Evaluation.   2. Elementary education
of adults—Iowa—Evaluation.   3. Adult education—Iowa—Evaluation.
I. Title.
    LC152.I8B43 1991
    374.9777—dc20   90–44263
                                                                          CIP

10   9   8   7   6   5   4   3   2

CONTENTS

PREFACE

For reasons which will become apparent as this volume progresses, in recent years adult literacy has become an issue of major concern in this nation. Yet despite the importance of this issue, much of the research based information about it is fragmentary and even contradictory. This is a major problem because in dealing with issues of program goals, eligibility for service, and the effective delivery of service, policy makers can benefit from the guidance which systematic inquiry can provide. Similarly, teachers need to know how best to educate and administrators must know how best to successfully attract to their programs voluntary learners. While no volume can provide definitive answers to these issues, there is a considerable literature which can at least inform practice. Being fragmented, however, the literature requires synthesis, and contradictions need to be resolved if research based knowledge is to have utility. It is my intent here to review what is known about the adult literacy population, and, in doing so, to shed light on the issues which must be addressed if practice is to be improved.

Although I have long been interested in the field of adult literacy, my motivation for writing this book began in 1986 with the first of what have become known as the Iowa Adult Literacy Studies. Although policy makers and planners in Iowa had a wealth of knowledge derived from experience, many additional questions of program effectiveness could be resolved only through systematic research. To start with, these policy makers wished to know what motivated adult basic education (ABE) students to attend literacy programs so that recruitment strategies which appealed to learners' motivations could be planned. These educators were also concerned with program effectiveness and with whether instruction was meeting the needs of particular groups of students.

The first of the Iowa Studies proved to be very useful, and consequently policy makers decided to continue with an expanded research program. The second study, which replicated the methodology of the first, focused on English as a second language (ESL) students. The third focused on those eligible for ABE who had never participated; it sought to determine the basic reasons for nonparticipation.

From the outset, the Iowa studies were conducted in close collaboration with policy makers, teachers, and administrators. Jane Sellen of Western Iowa Tech served as the project director and coordinated the logistics. John Hartwig of the State Department of Education maintained communication among staff members; Thomas Valentine of the University of Georgia and I were the principal investigators.

Taken as a whole these three studies provided an extremely comprehensive picture of adult literacy education in Iowa, and we suspected that many lessons had been learned which could be of value to professionals nationally. To test our suspicions, in 1989 a national panel of state ABE officials, researchers, and practitioners was asked to react to the Iowa Studies, and it became clear that much of what we had found had relevance elsewhere. However, in evaluating the value of the Iowa studies to others, we were faced with the problem of broader generalization. Just how much of what we had learned held true outside Iowa? There were only two ways to find out: to replicate the studies nationally, which would have involved considerable expense, or to compare our findings with other research to see where there were commonalities and where the Iowa work diverged. The second approach seemed feasible.

This volume, then, is an attempt to synthesize what we learned in Iowa with other high quality work conducted in other contexts. My ultimate goal was twofold. On one hand I wished to identify policy issues raised by research on adult literacy and to recommend solutions where warranted. On the other hand, I wanted to examine adult literacy education from the perspective of the learners themselves in order to inform improved practice. Whether or not I have been successful is for you the reader to judge.

There are many different ways I could have focused this book. I might have concentrated on teaching-learning transactions, for example, or attempted to provide a truly comprehensive picture of adult literacy education touching on all facets. I have chosen, however, to focus on the clients of adult literacy education—low literate adults. My treatment addresses six basic questions which constitute the topics of the first six chapters: What is adult literacy and adult literacy education? What factors define and describe the adult literacy population? What motivates adult literacy students to attend? Why do many of those eligible for adult literacy education elect not to participate? What are the outcomes and impact of adult literacy education, and what are the implications of the analysis for adult literacy and policy?

In reviewing the literature on adult literacy, I have made a systematic attempt to relate what we know about adult literacy to what we know about adult education participation in general. Furthermore, to elucidate rather than confuse, I have been purposefully selective, for as Fingeret (1984) notes:

> The literature in adult literacy education is voluminous, conveying the image of a substantive and useful knowledge base. However, a glance through an extensive bibliography, such as that generated through a thorough ERIC search, leaves the reader immersed in acronyms and discrete, site-specific reports that are difficult to relate to each other or to the planning of future efforts. In addition, the literature is spread over a range of disciplinary perspectives, confounding the difficulty of addressing such specific questions as "how do adults read?"(p. 3).

To: Tom Valentine, Jane Sellen and John Hartwig
for what we learned together.

CHAPTER 1

Introduction

In recent years the topic of adult literacy has received considerable attention. Although estimates of illiteracy vary greatly, we are told that as many as 60 million adults may be functionally illiterate in the United States, (Kozol, 1985) and that our national productivity and place in the world are at stake unless we improve our literacy rate. While twenty-five years ago adult literacy was a rather esoteric subject, today it is a matter of popular concern. Why has the issue of adult literacy become so prominent? There are at least two reasons. First, as knowledge has expanded in amount and complexity in the wake of technological growth, the sophistication required to be literate has increased accordingly. Thus, while adults were considered to be literate in the nineteenth century if they could write their names, and were deemed to be literate in the 1930s if they had achieved eighth grade, today adults are considered functionally illiterate unless they have mastered the complexities of technical manuals, tax forms, and the like. Second, literacy has been linked to worker productivity, and productivity has become a critical issue as this nation's economic prominence in the world is increasingly threatened.

To simply note that adult illiteracy is a problem gets us nowhere, however. The issue is what to do about the problem, and before we can solve that it is necessary to understand what literacy is, how it is defined both conceptually and in practice.

WHAT IS LITERACY?

Simply defined, literacy is the ability to read and write. Yet when this simple definition is examined, many complexities emerge.

1

The first problem is how to determine whether or not a given person is literate. This is obviously important in determining who needs literacy and who is eligible for literacy programs. One possibility is to use an absolute standard such as the completion of, or the ability to perform at, a particular grade level. Another possibility is to define literacy in terms of a set of skills. Bormouth (1975), for example, proposes a taxonomy of seven skills which relate to decoding, literal comprehension, inference, critical reading, aesthetic appreciation, reading flexibility, and study skills. However, many believe that being literate is relative rather than absolute, that attaining literacy is not simply attaining a collection of learned skills.

According to those who hold literacy to be relative, being literate depends on the specific literacy tasks posed by a particular situation or environment. As Scribner and Cole (1981) state, "Literacy is not simply knowing how to read and write a particular script but applying this knowledge for specific purposes in specific contexts of use" (p. 236). Hunter and Harman (1979) believe that "all definitions of literacy or illiteracy are completely relative" (p. 10). They define two kinds of literacy: conventional literacy, which is the "ability to read, write, and comprehend texts on familiar subjects and to understand whatever signs, labels, instructions, and directions are necessary to get along within one's environment," and functional literacy, "the possession of skills perceived as necessary by particular persons and groups to fulfill their own self-determined objectives . . . " (p .7). As Cervero notes (1985), while use of grade levels or other absolute definitions may be misleading, relativistic definitions require educators to teach different skills for each different context, and this is extremely difficult to do.

Just as opinions have differed about the definition of literacy, so have they differed about the goals and forms of literacy. Most commenters would agree that literacy includes more than mere reading and writing. For example, Scribner (1984), who focuses on the cultural aspects of literacy formation, notes three distinct social perceptions of literacy: literacy as adaptation, literacy as grace, and literacy as power. Literacy as adaptation stresses its pragmatic value, the proficiency needed for functioning in specific situations. Literacy as a state of grace assumes that literacy endows the literate person with special virtues and qualities such as being "cultured" or being wise. Literacy as power looks at the relationship between literacy, social mobility, and the maintenance of the hegemony of the elite.

In the literacy as power tradition, Giroux notes "Literacy is best understood as a myriad of discursive forms and cultural competencies that construct, and make available the various relations and experiences, that exist between learners and the world" (Freire & Macedo, 1987, p. 10). In learning to understand the socially constructed meanings which govern their behavior, illiterates become empowered to change the situations which have previously controlled them.

Freire and Macedo posit five approaches to literacy. The first, termed the academic approach, derives from classical notions of the well-educated person and focuses on mastering classical literature and highly abstract material. The authors claim that this is alienating for adult literacy learners, as it is divorced from the language and experience of the students. The second approach is the utilitarian approach which focuses on the reading requirements of society or groups and is closely akin to functional literacy. This is criticized for being a far too mechanistic approach which fails to entail a critical assessment of the society which determines reading needs. In the cognitive development approach, the construction of meaning is stressed in the problem solving process. "Comprehension of the text is relegated to a position of lesser importance in favor of the development of new cognitive structures that can enable students to move from simple to highly complex reading tasks" (p. 148). The fourth approach to literacy is termed the romantic approach, and it stresses the enriching value of reading, the pleasure it brings, and its ability to broaden one's mind.

The fifth approach to literacy, the one advocated by Freire and Macedo, is termed emancipatory literacy. In this tradition, literacy is seen as one of the mechanisms through which adults come to understand their world and, through the process of becoming literate, become empowered to act rather than being acted upon. While most other approaches to literacy concentrate on individual gain, emancipatory literacy focuses on social transformation—the elimination of dominant class hegemony and oppression. As Freire and Macedo state, "In this view, literacy programs should be tied not only to mechanical learning of reading skills but, additionally, to a critical understanding of the overall goals for national reconstruction. Thus, the reader's development of a critical comprehension of the text, and the sociohistorical context to which it refers, becomes an important factor in our notion of literacy" (p. 157).

In contrast to those who espouse an emancipatory approach

to literacy is the conservative approach of E. D. Hirsch (1987) who has coined the term *cultural literacy*. According to Hirsch, to be literate entails the mastering of material which is embodied in the shared meanings of society. "Society" is defined in terms of a national culture which includes such things as standard English, a commonly held interpretation of history, and the basic principles of science. This, according to Hirsch, is vital because the shared meanings of national culture are the basic context, or "schema," which enables learners to derive meaning from what they read. Thus, while for Freire and Macedo meaning is derived from the critical reflection of what is read in relation to the learner's perception of reality—a reality derived from the ongoing critical assessment of experience— for Hirsch meaning is derived from becoming an integral part of the very culture Freire and Macedo would seek to transform.

Overlaid on the discussion of what being literate means is the distinction between basic literacy and functional literacy. Basic literacy is generally defined as the ability to master the skills of reading and writing and to perform basic numerical computations. It tends to view literacy as a set of generalized skills. That is to say, once individuals can "read," they will be able to read in any context. Functional literacy is a bit more complex.

In the early 1970s, functional literacy was defined primarily as survival skills, literacy skills one needed to perform the daily tasks of life such as reading labels and filling out forms (Mezirow, Darkenwald, & Knox, 1975). However, in the mid-1970s functional literacy was given a slightly different meaning by the federally funded Adult Performance Level Project (APL). APL defined functional literacy in terms of "the competencies which are functional to economic and educational success in today's society" (Adult Performance Level Project, 1975, p. 1). APL identified five competency areas: consumer economics, occupational knowledge, health, community resources, and government and law. To identify skills necessary for success in these areas, the project employed a methodology which relied on a literature review, a survey of federal agencies and foundations, conferences with opinion leaders, and interviews with undereducated and unemployed adults. According to APL's critics, this methodology resulted in a distinct bias in which the competencies for effective functioning in society were defined in terms of what middle class adults were able to do effectively in contrast to what undereducated adults were not able to do (Griffith & Cervero, 1977).

As Valentine (1986b) aptly notes, to adequately define functional literacy it is necessary to consider two elements: learners' abilities and the literacy demands of the reference group in which learners are expected to function. This becomes exceedingly difficult given the almost infinite number of reference groups. From a practical point of view, this problem is being played out in workplace literacy which might be defined as functional literacy in one's place of employment. As Sticht and Mikulecky (1984) and others have shown, it is quite possible to develop a functional literacy curriculum for a learner's specific occupational role in a specific place of employment. Yet, given the great diversity in role and setting, this approach to literacy is expensive and time consuming, and learners may find it difficult to generalize beyond the workplace the literacy skills learned.

The relationship between "print" literacy and functional literacy may further confound definition. Valentine (1986a) notes that the term *functional literacy* generally refers to literacy which is "useful." Yet utility has three different meanings. First, some contend that ability to read print is inherently useful and thus functional literacy is synonymous with print literacy. The second meaning defines functional literacy as "print literacy which has instrumental value in adult life" (p. 18). In this case the objective is to teach learners to read print that enables more than affective or leisure outcomes. Although the third meaning does not ignore print, it goes beyond reading itself to include other skills that have instrumental value such as problem solving and interpersonal skills.

Although the debate over literacy definitions and goals is often confusing and chaotic, it is still possible to define literacy in a way that is compatible with most of the above definitions. Csikszentmihalyi (1990) states, "The ability to code and decode information stored in such extrasomatic memory systems is what we call literacy. A person who is literate has access to the knowledge stored in a particular system. A person may be the greatest genius, and may have learned from experience more than any other person knows, yet still be an illiterate if the only knowledge he or she has access to is the one stored in his or her brain. Thus illiterates are not necessarily less knowledgeable, less intelligent, or less able than their literate counterparts. But they are excluded from the network of information mediated by symbols. Whether this is a great handicap or not depends on the extent to which one must rely on such mediated knowledge to function well in a particular society" (p. 120).

Put more simply, literacy can be defined as the ability to derive meaning from knowledge stored in symbolic form. Accordingly, basic literacy may be defined as the ability to derive meaning from print. Functional literacy may be defined as the ability to derive meaning from the codified knowledge specific to a particular context, and emancipatory literacy can be defined as the ability to derive meaning from the codifications of society itself. Clearly, such a definition of literacy crosscuts most others, and this is an advantage. More importantly, however, such a definition recognizes that, regardless of social status, everyone is illiterate to a certain degree. Many of my highly educated colleagues, for example, are computer illiterates, and I am semi-illiterate when it comes to comprehending nineteenth century German philosophy. Thus illiteracy, so defined, starts to become disembedded from social stigma.

The discussion about what literacy is raises several issues for policy at the local, state, and federal levels. The first deals with the question of whether being literate is an absolute or whether it is relative. If it is absolute, if there is a definable state of being literate which is independent of the literacy tasks imposed by specific literacy contexts, then a nationally standardized literacy curriculum is possible. Analogous to the curricula of elementary and secondary education, such a curriculum would teach basically the same material regardless of program location. It would also be possible to establish common accountability standards for measuring progress such as standardized tests or advances in grade level. However, if literacy is relative, and if being literate depends on how well learners perform the literacy tasks required of specific situations, programs must be developed for each literacy context. It also follows that the acquisition of literacy could not be assessed by any common measure, and that a standardized curriculum, or anything close to it, would be anathema.

It is quite possible that there is some truth in both positions, that there are cultural norms for "being literate" which support a more or less absolute definition roughly equivalent to grade levels, and that, in addition, specific situations also require specialized literacy skills. Yet if both positions have merit, does a national literacy program need to address both in order to be adequate, and, if so, how would such a program be constituted?

A second issue pertains to the social role of literacy. Notions of basic literacy and APL's conception of functional literacy focus on individual skill development which presumably helps learners to rise in the socioeconomic system by earning more and investing increments of income in things which benefit both society and themselves. But is individual skill development sufficient? A progressive notion of adult education (Elias & Merriam, 1980) would argue that the informed participation of all citizens is necessary if democracy is to work. As Bergevin (1967, p. 35) states, "There is little doubt that, if democracy is to survive, citizens must participate intelligently in the affairs of various institutions that constitute democratic society. And intelligent participation is predicated on learning." Should adult literacy education focus more on collective civic participation?

While Freire (1970) and the advocates of emancipatory literacy would answer in the affirmative, they would go a step further to assist the low literate in developing the kind of critical consciousness which results in collective action directed toward social transformation. In their view it is society which produces illiteracy rather than individuals, and the problem of illiteracy cannot be addressed unless the social order itself is transformed.

A third issue pertains to what the content of literacy education should be and who should decide. Following a basic literacy approach, should literacy education focus simply on basic reading, writing, and computational skills assuming that once deficiencies have been remediated individuals will be able to make over their own lives? Or should we focus on functional literacy in the workplace so that learners will gain what they need to function in a specific milieu with the added benefit of enhanced job performance? Based on the premise that they are the guardians of the common good, should policy makers decide what the content of adult literacy education should be? Or should such decisions be left to experts, who by virtue of their education and training are presumed to know what learners need to learn and how to teach it? Perhaps learners themselves should determine the content of adult literacy education. After all, unlike children, adults are responsible for their own actions and are fully capable of making choices about what they wish to learn.

Are the shared meanings of the national culture the real meat of literacy? Quite possibly adults need to understand the national culture if they are to negotiate it, but who will decide what constitutes the national culture—the very people who have used it in hegemonic ways for their own benefit? Perhaps all of the above are wrong. Perhaps literacy should be viewed not as a set of contents but as a process through which adults learn to critically assess their world and, in doing so, transform it.

ADULT LITERACY EDUCATION

Although different conceptions of literacy raise important issues that need to be considered, from a pragmatic standpoint it makes sense to define a literacy program according to what the program does. Literacy education in the United States consists of three overlapping systems. The first is a tutor based system represented by such organizations as Laubach Literacy Action and Literacy Volunteers of America. These organizations train layperson volunteers who are assigned to tutor low literate clients. Generally the instruction takes place in a non-school site such as a library or the tutor's home, although in some cases tutors assist in formal classroom oriented programs. Both Laubach Literacy Action and Literacy Volunteers of America publish instructional materials for students' and tutors' use, and these materials are occasionally used in formal programs. According to government data (Pugsley, 1990), the volunteer sector of adult literacy education has expanded rapidly in recent years to the extent that in 1988 volunteers constituted 40% of the teaching staff in the federal adult literacy program.

The second system is comprised of community based organizations. Hamilton and Cunningham (1990, p. 439) note that "The common organizational elements that characterize most of these are local initiative, control, maintenance, evaluation, and program development." Community based organizations develop from the community to solve community problems such as illiteracy. They tend to focus on collective action rather than on individual gain, and many embrace an emancipatory literacy philosophy. Although some receive public funding, many do not. For most, literacy education is but one of their goals which range from health to environmental concerns.

In a study of 31 community based adult literacy programs, the Association for Community Based Education (1986a) identified several key characteristics of these programs. Community based adult literacy programs typically are geared toward holistic change in individuals, and literacy is often conceived as an important means toward broad based community and economic development. They tend to serve the harder-to-reach student, and they often employ group oriented, participatory, teaching-learning methods. For community based programs, "Literacy is a means to a larger end—the ability to better control one's own life, or to contribute to the life of the community" (p. 25). Most programs are not located in public schools. An examination of program profiles of community based literacy programs (Association for Community Based Education, 1986b) indicates that while many receive some public funding, most are also supported by private contributions.

The third system, which is by far the largest, is the publicly funded adult literacy program first established by the federal government as part of the war on poverty in 1964 and reconstituted by the Adult Education Act of 1966 (Title III of the 1966 Amendments to the Elementary and Secondary Act). In 1988, programs funded by the Adult Education Act served 3 million adult students (Pugsley, 1990).

The federal program, which is supplemented with state funds in most localities, has three basic components (Taylor, 1990): English as a second language (ESL) which focuses on teaching English to those who can not speak the language, adult secondary education (ASE), and adult basic education (ABE). Since the clientele and technology of teaching ESL differ substantially from the other components of the federal program, in practice the ESL component is often considered to be a separate entity. Adult secondary education in most states is geared to preparing learners to pass the GED tests, and ABE is considered to be instruction at the less than high school level. To confuse the definition, however, at times ABE has been used to refer to the entire federal program, and in many regions there is little distinction in practice between ABE and GED preparation.

For two reasons it is difficult to portray accurately what adult literacy education is like at the local level. First, programming varies considerably by state and locale so that it is difficult to describe the "typical" adult literacy program. Second, with two notable exceptions—Fingeret's *North Carolina Adult Basic Education Evaluation 1985* (1985) and Mezirow, Darkenwald, and Knox's *Last Gamble on Education* (1975)—there is a lack of holistic, descriptive research that sensitizes the reader to the dynamics of adult literacy education. Nevertheless it is possible to identify several themes from the literature which crosscut adult literacy education in the United States: programmatic pluralism, common professional norms, and the teaching-learning technology.

Programmatic Pluralism

The delivery system for adult literacy can best be described as being pluralistic in that different states and localities have responded to the need to provide instruction in a multitude of ways. A pluralistic delivery system has resulted for at least two reasons. First, the provision of adult literacy education has always been conceived in federal policy as a state responsibility (Huang, Benavot, & Cervero, 1990) and there is little in the Adult Education Act which has restricted states to a particular delivery system (Beder, 1979).

Second, local situations vary considerably, and delivery systems have evolved over time which fit local conditions. There are many examples. In the early 1970s, New York targeted urban populations as its major priority. Consequently, a large proportion of its literacy resources was allocated toward establishing comprehensive urban adult learning centers. On the other hand, while most other states rely heavily on the public schools for their delivery systems, several states such as Iowa and North Carolina chose community colleges. Because of high population density and a good transportation infrastructure, New Jersey has established learning centers in its urban areas which are staffed by full time professionals and operate for twelve hours a day. In the outlying suburban areas, however, evening classes taught by part time teachers are the norm. A similar situation exists in North Carolina (Fingeret, 1985). In areas where a community college is located, learning centers are logistically feasible, while in the hinterlands a one room schoolhouse approach is used. Some states with large rural populations, such as Wisconsin (Beder & Darkenwald, 1974), have experimented with distance education.

Thus the various options for delivering adult literacy education—evening classes, learning centers, tutors, distance education, computer based education—are found in different configurations depending on the circumstances. If there is a commonality, it derives from the relationship between adult literacy education and the public schools. Since the Adult Education Act was part of the Elementary and Secondary Education Act Amendments of 1966, it was only natural that states would turn to the public schools as the focus of their delivery systems, and this occurred in the great majority of states. Most publicly funded adult literacy programs are administered by public schools and most classes are still conducted in public schools. In addition, in the early days of the federal program there were no commonly accepted adult literacy technologies to draw upon, and thus adult literacy educators turned to elementary and secondary schools for their educational models.

Common Professional Norms

Although the work of Fingeret (1985) and Mezirow, Darkenwald, and Knox (1975) was conducted at different times and with different populations, there is great similarity in the authors' descriptions of the professional norms of those who work in publicly funded adult literacy programs. Professional norms derive from educators' perceptions regarding the purpose of adult literacy education and beliefs and attitudes about adult literacy students.

In her North Carolina study, Fingeret notes that administrators and teachers alike perceive the purpose of adult literacy to be the "mainstreaming" of learners whose social mobility has been limited for lack of literacy. Similarly, in their study of inner city literacy programs, Mezirow, Darkenwald, and Knox report that teachers rank "increased ability to cope with adult real life and problems" and "increased self-confidence" as more important than the traditional goals of adult literacy such as "increased competency in language skills" and "preparation for the high school equivalency exam." More than being guardians of knowledge or transmitters of skills, teachers consider themselves to be guides, guides who are remediating the dysfunctions which they believe limit learners' access to middle class society.

The norms associated with "guiding," however, are mediated by at least two factors. First, adult literacy education is a voluntary activity and little can be achieved unless learners stick with it. In the wake of large dropout rates, teachers place a great deal of emphasis on "holding" students. This results in what Mezirow et al. term the "ideology of minimum failure." They state, "Although the structure of the institutional process is traditional, the process itself has been modified to define failure as such out of existence in the classroom and minimize its increments in teacher-student interaction. The only failure becomes the failure to come to class. And of course, the pressure to maintain attendance substantially fosters the ideology of minimum failure" (p. 30).

Professional norms, then, focus on minimizing student failure, and the voluntary nature of adult literacy education leads teachers to believe it is necessary to do so. Yet there is a second factor which mediates guiding that is also important and it pertains to how teachers *perceive* their students. Fingeret vividly portrays such perceptions: "Descriptions of students provide insight into the underlying assumptions and beliefs that guide the decisions and actions of instructors. A close examination of these descriptions yields a complex image. On one hand, students are described as 'motivated,' 'talented,' 'determined,' 'street-wise,' and 'goal-oriented.' Students are described as participating in the face of adversity and sacrifice. However, equally consistent are descriptions of students who are insecure about their ability to succeed with academic work, have a terrible 'self-concept,' and see themselves as failures, generally" (p. 81).

In belief that students' self-concepts are frail and based on past failure, Fingeret notes that teachers often adopt a condescending stance toward them. To guide successfully, teachers believe they must nurture and establish a family atmosphere, for otherwise students will be driven from the program. For students who seem likely to fail, "trying hard" and "sticking with it" are more important than skill acquisition. As Mezirow et al. note, teachers with warm and accepting personalities are sought for the guiding mission; rigid and authoritarian types are avoided.

Although the "ideology of minimum failure" and professional norms which favor nurturing over skill acquisition seem to be quite pervasive, it is important to note that such norms do not apply in all cases. Indeed, the emancipatory education philosophy which characterizes many community based programs is inimical to such norms.

Teaching-Learning Technology

The teaching-learning technology of most publicly funded programs is strongly influenced by the public schools. Many teachers have been trained as elementary or secondary school teachers and have taught in public schools (Martin & Fisher, 1990). The substantial socialization they have received for the teacher role carries over to their work with adults. Furthermore, most of the materials used in adult literacy education are based on elementary and secondary models, although most publishers have included adult oriented content. Instructional materials strongly influence the teaching-learning technology, for, as Fingeret notes (1985), the materials become the method in most adult literacy classrooms. The strong reliance on materials in teaching is abetted by the fact that the vast majority of teachers work part time in adult literacy (Pugsley, 1990) and do not have the time to plan deviations from the structure provided by materials. Similarly, many programs employ paraprofessional volunteers who, lacking training in education, must rely on these materials to teach.

Most adult literacy programs permit open enrollment; students come and leave throughout the "semester." In addition, when a classroom model is used there are often wide variations in the levels and abilities of students. Consequently, instruction is typically individualized (Fingeret, 1985) and personalized (Mezirow, Darkenwald, & Knox, 1975). In classroom models teachers individualize in five basic ways (Mezirow et al., 1975). Sometimes they take turns with individual students. Sometimes they "search out" students who seem to be having difficulty. Some teachers expect needy students to volunteer for individual help; others have students help each other, and still others assign volunteers to individual assistance. In learning center models, all instruction is typically individualized and students work at their own pace with sequenced materials seeking help when they need it.

Adult literacy education, then, can be viewed from two perspectives. On one hand there is a tapestry of diversity brought about by differing programmatic adaptations to differing local conditions. On the other hand, there are distinct commonalities which result from common professional norms and the affiliation with public schools. Certainly there are differences between the tutor based, community based, and federal program sectors. Yet the fact that all adult literacy students are voluntary learners who experience similar life problems provides a continuity.

THE ADULT EDUCATION ACT

While norms of behavior have an obvious effect at the local level, the entire federal adult literacy endeavor is strongly affected by national policy which is embodied in the Adult Education Act. The Adult Education Act has been amended sixteen times since 1966 (Legislative history, PL 100–297, Elementary and Secondary School Improvement Amendments of 1988). The purpose of the current law is quite revealing and worth quoting in entirety.

> It is the purpose of this title to assist the States to improve educational opportunities for adults who lack the level of literacy skills requisite to effective citizenship and productive employment, to expend and improve the current system for delivering adult education services including the delivery of such services to educationally disadvantaged adults, and to encourage the establishment of adult education programs which will—
>
> (1) enable these adults to acquire the basic educational skills for literate functioning;
>
> (2) provide these adults with sufficient basic education to benefit from job training and retraining programs and obtain and retain effective employment so that they might more fully enjoy the benefits and responsibilities of citizenship; and
>
> (3) enable adults who might so desire to continue their education to at least the level of completion of secondary school.

Clearly it is the intent of the act to extend literacy based schooling to those adults who have missed it, but for what purpose? The answer is in part revealed in the statement "to benefit from job training and retraining programs and . . . retain productive employment." To a large extent the justification for the federal adult literacy program rests in a human capital argument which goes something like this: National productivity, and indeed security, depends on an educated workforce which is able to perform the sophisticated tasks required by technological complexity. Hence, investments in adult literacy represent social benefits. That is to say that, although individual learners benefit, a large part of the investment in adult literacy accrues to society as a whole in terms of the increased national wealth which productivity affords.

Although human capital was always a rationale for public funding, this argument seems to have been strengthened in the 1988 amendments which provide for an allocation of 30 million dollars to pay 70% of the costs of workplace literacy programs conducted in partnership with businesses, industry, labor organizations, or private industry councils. Workplace literacy, so defined, goes well beyond basic literacy to include such things as upgrading skills needed in the workplace and improving competency in speaking, listening, reasoning, and problem solving.

The term "adult" is defined in the act as an *individual* who is age 16 and is beyond compulsory schooling, and adult education is defined as instruction for those "who lack sufficient mastery of basic educational skills to enable them to function effectively in society" and whose lack of skills results in an impairment of their ability to retain employment. The program is designed to reduce such impairment "with a view of making them less dependent on others."

For right or for wrong, the language of the act seems to be consistent with the professional norms described earlier. The purpose of the act is to remedy individual deficiencies and impairments which limit employment and effective functioning. For lack of literacy, students are seen as being dependent, and that dependence must be corrected for the health of the total society.

Several other provisions of the act merit comment. While public or private nonprofit agencies are eligible for funding, they can be funded only if the applicable local educational agency has been consulted and has had the opportunity to comment. This clearly favors local educational agencies as providers, as does the stipulation that at the state level the act is to be administered by state educational agencies which, in most cases, are the same agencies that administer the public schools.

The act stipulates that the federal share of expenditures will decline from 90% in fiscal year 1988 to 85% in fiscal year 1990, from 80% in 1991 to 75% in 1992. The intent here is to induce states to increase their allocations to adult literacy thus increasing the total amount of funds available for the program.

Not more than 20% of a state's allocation may be spent on high school equivalency, despite the fact that in such states as Iowa (Beder & Valentine, 1987) and North Carolina (Fingeret, 1985), there is little distinction in practice between high school equivalency and lower grade level equivalency.

The 1988 Act authorizes grants to states to train adult volunteers to assist in literacy efforts, thus strengthening the relationship between ABE and volunteerism. According to Pugsley (1990), 74,626 volunteers were used in the 1988 federal adult basic education program and constituted 50% of the entire workforce.

For the first time in the history of the act, the 1988 amendments require that a state's program be evaluated according to standardized test data. The implications of this are significant. What standards of accountability will be applied to the performance of an adult learner? Will a comparison with the school performance of preadults become the standard, and, if this comparison does become the standard, are we not in danger of losing the adultness in adult literacy? Or will comparisons with other local programs' scores become the normative standard? If so, it becomes rational for programs to "cream" by screening out the least able learners who can be expected to show less gain on standard tests. If this results, who will serve those who need adult literacy the most?

The fiscal year 1990 budget for the Adult Education Act is as follows (Program Services Branch, 1990):

State grant program	$157.8 million
National special projects	2.0 million
Literacy for the homeless	7.4 million
Workplace literacy	19.7 million
ESL grant program	5.9 million
	$192.8 million

The federal allocation to adult literacy has nearly doubled since 1980 when the budget was 100 million dollars (Development Associates, 1980), and when state and local governments' allocations were added to the federal allotment the total increased 270 percent between 1980 and 1988 (Pugsley, 1990). Yet despite increases in funding, the publicly funded program is still serving only about 8% of the target population, and the average expenditure per student was but $160 in 1988 (Puglsey, 1990). Additional resources are clearly needed.

BASIC QUESTIONS

The preceding discussion raises four basic questions which will serve as guiding themes throughout this book, themes which will be addressed substantially in the sixth chapter: What should the goals and purposes of adult literacy education be? Who should be served? How can learners be attracted to programs, and how should adult literacy education be provided?

Goals and Purposes

What should the goals and purposes of adult literacy education be? Both the stated goals of the publicly funded program and prevalent professional norms suggest that the intent is to assist educationally and socially deficient adults to increase their social mobility— to help them to take their places in middle class society. As Fingeret (1984) notes, the focus is on the individual. Programs present the opportunity for advancement, and individuals are expected to seize the opportunity to their own benefit and that of society. Indeed, the entire teaching-learning technology of the federal program is based upon individual growth.

Individual growth and change, however, is only one option. In Latin America (Beder, 1989c), and in some community based programs (Hamilton & Cunningham, 1990; Fingeret, 1984), an emancipatory literacy approach is favored that focuses on assisting groups of low literate adults to change society rather than to fit into it. Should adult literacy be designed to serve a society which is basically just and good, or should it be conceived as a strategy to transform a society which is inherently unequal and therefore unjust? On this, the issue of goals and purposes partially turns.

Should adult literacy be conceived primarily as a program to benefit the economy, or should it focus on wider social benefit? If economic benefit is the answer, then it is rational to restrict instruction to the narrow range of literacy skills required for occupational productivity. But if wider social benefit is desired, the concept of literacy must be expanded to include knowledge and skills which improve the general quality of life. Quality of life skills and knowledge may go considerably beyond "functional" and "coping" skills to include things like aesthetic appreciation. Is the public willing to pay the price? Can we afford not to if the democratic order requires the informed, reasoned, participation of all citizens?

Who Should Be Served?

In exploring who should be served there are several options. We might, for example, concentrate on those who are most motivated to participate and are most likely to attend, the "demand population." This is the most efficient option, for focusing on the demand population does not require large investments in recruitment and new programming that might appeal to chronic nonparticipants. Unfortunately, however, those who enroll in adult literacy education are not necessarily the ones who need it the most, the most disadvantaged and the least literate. Although to focus on the greatest in need and hardest to reach may be technically possible, it may be much more expensive also. Given limited resources, focusing on the neediest could necessitate turning some of the most motivated away.

How Can Adult Learners Be Attracted?

While the goals and purposes of adult literacy and the question of who should be served are primarily value issues, the issue of how learners can be attracted is an empirical question. To answer it we need to better understand what motivates learners to attend and why nonparticipants elect not to attend. Clearly the problem is significant when only 8% of those eligible for the federal program attend (Pugsley, 1990).

It may be that current programs conceive literacy in terms which are too narrow to address the full range of factors which motivate low literate adults to become literate. It may also be that many potential learners simply do not feel they need literacy education or that they hold negative values and attitudes toward literacy education. Although these issues will be discussed in depth in Chapters Three and Four, it is important to recognize here that substantial modifications in the adult literacy system may be necessary if our performance in reaching the target population is to be substantially improved. It may also be that improved success will require us to focus policy much more on the needs and preferences of potential clients, and in doing so, to move away from the kind of "top-down" policy making which has characterized the federal effort to date.

How Should Adult Literacy Education Be Provided?

This question deals with the delivery system for adult literacy education. When some contemplate the great diversity of providers and programs which characterizes adult literacy education, they conclude that the system is fragmented and in great need of consolidation and coordination. However, when others view the same configuration of programs, they conclude that the system is pluralistic, that diversity is an asset which has resulted from the system's ability to adapt to local situations and needs. Should the delivery system maximize efficiency and accountability through greater standardization and coordination? Or should it maximize flexibility by permitting pluralism to flourish?

As has been noted, traditional literacy education programs operate on a deficit model. Low literates are viewed as being unable to function in society for lack of critical knowledge and skills. While this view provides the justificatory logic for public subsidy, it also supports the stigma which society attaches to illiteracy, a stigma which makes it all the more difficult for low literates to succeed. Is it possible for adult literacy education to eradicate the deficit orientation and still fulfill its mission?

CHAPTER 2

The Target Population: Who Are They?

DEFINITION AND ESTIMATION

How many adults in the United States are illiterate? Although this would seem to be a fundamental question for practice and policy in adult literacy education, there is no definitive answer. Estimates of adult literacy vary widely according to how the target population is defined. Indeed the issue of definition has so frustrated scholars that Hunter and Harman (1979) entitled their discussion of definition "Lies, Damned Lies, and Statistics" and Kozol (1985) entitled his analysis "Matters of Equivocation: Dangers of the Numbers Game." Yet despite wide variations in estimates of adult illiteracy, it is possible to make some sense of the definition problem.

Essentially there are three ways that the target population for adult literacy has been defined: according to adults' abilities to perform tasks necessary for functioning in society, according to their abilities to perform basic reading and computational tasks, and according to grade level attainment. The first way might be termed the functional competency approach, the second the functional reading approach, and the third the grade level approach.

The Adult Performance Level (APL) Project is an example of a research effort which has taken the functional competency approach to definition and population estimation (Adult Performance Level Project, 1975). Based on a review of the literature, surveys of public officials, conferences, and interviews with undereducated adults, APL developed a taxonomy of adult needs which fall into five content areas: consumer economics, occupational knowledge, community resources, health, and government and law. According to the researchers, four skills are needed to function within the content areas: communication skills, computation skills, problem solving skills, and interpersonal skills. APL then derived 65 objectives from its taxonomy which operationally define functional literacy.

To assess the adult literacy rate, five national studies were conducted using simulations based on the 65 objectives. Based on study results (Clearinghouse on Adult Education and Literacy, 1989), adults were grouped into three levels. The first category, "adults who function with difficulty," is, according to APL, associated with poverty, inadequate education and low level employment. It is estimated that 20% of the adult population falls into this group. The second category, "functional adults," is comprised of adults who are functioning, but barely. At this level, although income is above the poverty level, there is no discretionary income. The educational level of the second category is generally between 9 to 11 years, and occupational status is in the medial range. APL claims that 34% of the adult population is at the marginally proficient level two. APL's third category, "proficient adults," is made up of those who are fully functioning in society; they are estimated to comprise about 46% of the adult population. Thus, according to APL, over half of the adults in the United States have functional literacy problems and are in need of education to remedy them. More seriously, one fifth of all adults have severe problems in functioning and are in great need of adult "functional literacy" education.

Defining adult literacy from a functional reading perspective, Harris and associates (1971) asked a national sample of adults to answer questions based on reading such things as a newspaper, a telephone directory, and a job application. The authors concluded that about 15% of adults in the United States have serious reading problems. In 1976 the National Assessment of Educational Progress (NAEP) adopted a similar approach in its national study of adults aged 26 to 35. NAEP asked subjects to complete a series of basic skills exercises such as filling out a mail order form, using a tax table, and writing a job application letter. "The average percent correct for the entire nation on these exercises was 73%" (p. 1).

Additionally, NAEP found that performance was strongly influenced by educational level, income, race, and urban residence. For example, while those with graduate degrees performed correctly on 84% of NAEP's basic skills exercises, only 49% of those with nine or less years of school performed correctly. Although the correct response rate for those with incomes over $15,000 was 78%, the proportion of correct responses for those whose incomes were under $5,000 was but 57%.

The third method of defining the target population for adult literacy education, the grade level approach, is the most common, and this is so for very pragmatic reasons. Under the Adult Education Act, federal funds are allocated to the states according to the ratio of adults who lack a high school diploma to the total state population. Thus the use of grade level attainment to define the target population has its basis in the law. Furthermore, grade levels are easily determined from census data and they represent a precise criterion which can be applied nationally. Yet despite the efficiency of this method of defining the target population, there is an obvious weakness; grade level does not necessarily correspond to literacy level. In fact, there may be many adults who are quite literate despite failure to complete school and others, unfortunately, who are illiterate despite having graduated from secondary school.

Defining the target population for adult literacy education as persons age 16 and over who lack a high school diploma and who are out of school results in 51.8 million adults who are eligible for the federal program. Of this number, 3 million attended federally supported adult literacy education programs in 1988 (Pugsley, 1990). Grade levels are further used to distinguish within the target population. Adults who have attained eight grades of education or less are defined as level I; those who have attained between 9 and 12 years of schooling are termed level II.

Clearly, estimates of illiteracy rates vary according to how illiteracy is defined, and the more comprehensive the definition, the larger the estimate. Yet even by the most conservative estimates, illiteracy is a major problem in the United States. Given this conclusion, it is important to identify the factors which affect participation in adult literacy programs and to understand how the target population for adult literacy education differs from the general population.

SOCIOECONOMIC STATUS

As the APL, NAEP, and many other studies show, there is a strong relationship between adult illiteracy and low socioeconomic status as defined by income, occupational status, and educational attainment. However defined, the adult literacy population is poorer, less educated, and employed in jobs of lower status than the general population. In turn, socioeconomic status is related to participation in all forms of adult education including adult literacy education. The lower the socioeconomic status, the lower the rate of participation.

The first large scale study to explore the relationship between participation in adult education and socioeconomic variables was Johnstone and Rivera's (1965) classic, *Volunteers for Learning.* The national study was conducted on a probability sample of 11,957 households which encompassed 23,950 adults. Education was defined broadly to include "all activities consciously and systematically organized for purposes of acquiring new knowledge, information, or skills" (p. 1).

Johnstone and Rivera estimated that one fifth of the adults in the United States had participated in adult education in the year prior to June 1962. Yet participation rates were found to vary considerably according to socioeconomic status variables, particularly education. As the authors state, "By far the most persistent finding in our investigation was that formal educational attainment plays a highly critical role in determining whether or not one enters the ranks of adult students. Better educated students were found not only to be more active in learning pursuits, but also more interested in learning per se, more ready to turn to formal instruction to satisfy interests, and much more knowledgeable about the existence of resources for continuing education" (p. 21).

Johnstone and Rivera found that while 32% of adult education participants were white collar workers, only 17% were blue collar workers. Although 29% of the adults in higher income levels participated, only 12% of those in the lowest income levels participated. The participation rate for adults with a grade school education was 6%; the rate for those with college years was 38% (p. 97).

While Johnstone and Rivera argued convincingly that participation in adult education was strongly influenced by socioeconomic status, they were unable to identify precisely the relative impact of socioeconomic variables or to set up control for the interrelationships among socioeconomic variables. Anderson and Darkenwald (1979) rectified these problems. To determine what factors best distinguished adult education participants from nonparticipants, the researchers analyzed adult education participation data collected by the National Center for Educational Statistics using multiple regression analysis. The sample consisted of responses from nearly 80,000 adults age 17 or older.

Anderson and Darkenwald found that the most powerful predictor of participation in adult education was formal schooling and that this effect of formal schooling was independent of other socioeconomic variables such as income and occupation. Age was the second most important predictor, with participation declining as age increased. Most important, however, were the authors' findings of what did not predict participation. They state, "Family income appears to have little effect on participation in adult education. Low income adults are under represented among participants, but this is mainly caused by other factors associated with poverty such as low educational attainment" (p. 4). Likewise, black racial status had little impact on participation when such factors as low educational attainment were controlled.

Taken together, all socioeconomic variables accounted for only 10% of the variance in participation. In addition, adult literacy students were found to be four times more likely to drop out of adult education than other students. Anderson and Darkenwald's analysis highlights a major problem facing adult literacy educators. Adults with less education are the least likely to seek more of it. Thus, more than for other forms of adult education, recruiting and retaining learners is critical for program success.

DESCRIPTIVE PROFILE

Sociodemographics

As noted in the previous chapter, adult literacy education in the United States can be divided into three overlapping systems, a tutor based system through which students are instructed by volunteer tutors, a community based system, and the federal program. While sociodemographic data is not available for the tutor and community based systems, the government has systematically compiled data on the federal program which in 1988 enrolled 3 million students (Pugsley, 1990). Thus is it possible to describe the sociodemographic characteristics of those enrolled in the federal program according to educational level, age, race, gender, economic status, and regional differences.

Educational level

According to the 1980 census, there are 51.8 million adults in the United States age 16 and over who are out of school and who lack a high school diploma. Of these, 25.6 million (49%) attained between 9 and 12 years of schooling, and 26.2 million (51%) attained eight or less years of schooling. This represents the federal target population for adult literacy education. Clearly there is considerable variation in educational level within the target population, and this affects participation rates, as participation in adult literacy education increases as educational level increases. It follows that without some controls the most poorly educated adults are likely to be underserved by the federal program. In recognition of this situation, the Adult Education Act prohibits states from spending more than 20% of their federal funds on adult secondary education, defined as instruction for those at the grade 9 to 12 level.

Despite the 20% prohibition, however, the greater demand for adult secondary education seems to have prevailed. Russ-Eft and McLaughlin (1981) report a participation rate for adult literacy students at the 10th and 11th grade level which is almost twice that of those at the 8th grade level, and the government reports that in 1988, 65% of those served were at the zero to 8th grade level, and 35% were at the 9th to 12th grade level (Office of Vocational and Adult Education, 1989). The disparity between the desired and actual ratio points to a serious problem which Mezirow, Darkenwald, and Knox (1975) term "creaming." Because more educated students are easier to attract to adult literacy programs, and because funding allocations are to a large extent based on the size of enrollment, there is a tendency to serve the more educated to the detriment, perhaps, of those who have the least education.

Age

1980 census data shows that 8% of the target population are between age 16 and 24; 18% are between age 25 and 44; 23% are between age 45 and 59, and 51% are 60 and over. Clearly, age is a powerful defining characteristic, and the fact that the majority of those who lack high school credentials are over 60 years of age demonstrates the impact of educational opportunity. Educational opportunity has varied considerably over the past 50 years. For many of those who were of school age in the 1920s through the 1940s, secondary school was simply not available and was less important for occupational success. As Heisel and Larson (1984) demonstrate, however, many of those who did not attend secondary school in bygone eras have learned to read on their own and are quite literate in a functional sense.

When the ages of those who actually participate in the federal program are examined, however, large disparities between the target population and participants are evident. In fiscal year 1988, 38% of the actual participants were age 16 to 24; 44% were age 24 to 44; 11% were age 45 to 59, and only 6% were age 60 or over (Pugsley, 1990). Quite obviously the federal program predominantly serves the younger segment of the target population. Although this is quite understandable, given that participation in adult education in general declines sharply with age (Anderson & Darkenwald, 1979), it is also quite clear that age is the most important variable in demarcating the demand population for adult literacy education—those who are most likely to participate. Perhaps this situation is desirable. After all, younger adults have many years of their productive lives left, productivity which adult literacy education may enhance to the benefit of the entire society. Yet it is disturbing to note that such a large proportion of the target population, over half, is not being adequately served by adult literacy education. Does failure to reach older adults represent an unacceptable social cost?

Race

Census data shows that 72% of the federal target population for adult literacy education are Caucasian, 14% are black, 11% are Hispanic, and 2% are Asian or native American. Of those who par-

ticipated in the federal program, 39% were Caucasian, 17% were
black, 32% were Hispanic, and 12% were Asian or native American
(Office of Vocational and Adult Education, 1989). Adult literacy
education has apparently been quite successful in reaching ethnic
minorities, and this may be due to the fact that reaching minorities
has been a federal priority since the inception of the Adult Education
Act in 1966.

Gender

Federal data for the 1988 program year indicates that 46% of
the adult literacy education participants are males, and 54% are
female (Pugsley, 1990). This ratio has been quite stable since the
1984–1985 program year (Pugsley, 1990) and does not differ substantially from the gender ratios for participation in adult education
in general which in 1984 were 55% for females and 45% for males
(Hill, 1987). The percentage of females who participate in the program appears to increase with age. While the majority of adult literacy students are males (51%) in the 16 to 24 age group, females
predominate in the 25 to 44 age group (53%) and increase to 59%
in the 54 to 59 age group and to 66% in the 60 and over age group
(Pugsley, 1987).

Economic Factors

Upon entering the federal adult literacy program, 39% of the
students held jobs in program year 1988 while 42% were unemployed, and 15% were on public assistance (Pugsley, 1990). Obviously the unemployment rate for adult literacy participants is well
above the national norm, and considerably above the rate for adults
who did not complete high school, which in 1986 was 15.4% (Pugsley, 1987). These figures are commendable given that a reduction
in unemployment is a stated objective of the federal program.

The incomes of the target population are strongly affected by
educational attainment and by gender. While the median income for
male college graduates was $30,298 in 1984, it was $12,529 for
adults with between one and three years of high school and $10,325
for adult males with eight grades of schooling. Obtaining a high
school diploma has a significant effect on income. In 1984 males
who had completed high school earned a median $18,825 as com-
pared to $12,529 for males with one to three years of high school.

Females fare considerably more poorly in respect to income. The 1984 median income for females with a college education was $13,484 as compared to $4,930 for women with between one and three years of high school and $4,657 for women with eight grades of school (Center for Educational Statistics, 1987).

Russ-Eft and Mclaughlin (1981) report that a greater proportion of those who participate in adult literacy education have incomes in the highest category than do the target population. Thus those who are likely to participant are more affluent than those who are eligible for adult literacy education but do not participate.

Regional Differences

There are considerable regional differences in the federal program in terms of who is served and in terms of how they are served. Literacy rates, for example, vary considerably, with states such as Mississippi, Louisiana, New York, and Texas having adult illiteracy rates of 16% and states such as Vermont, Utah and Iowa experiencing illiteracy rates in the range of 6 to 10% (Pugsley, 1990). The numbers served by the federal adult literacy program have increased substantially since 1968, with 455,000 students served in 1968, 1.8 million served in 1979, and 3 million served in 1988. Yet growth also varies by region. Between 1985 and 1986, for example, adult literacy education enrollment in the central states increased almost 40%, while enrollment in the southern states declined by 8% (Pugsley, 1987). While three fifths of the adult literacy students in the central states are Caucasian, a little over one third of the eastern students are Caucasian. Blacks constitute a fifth of those served in the east, but less than 2% of those served in the western states (Pugsley, 1987).

Per student expenditures also vary considerably. While the average cost per student was $160 in fiscal year 1987, for the eastern states it was $199 and for the southern states it was $131 (Pugsley, 1990).

Other Data

Government data indicates (Pugsley, 1987) that about one third of adult literacy participants come from urban areas of high unemployment and one quarter reside in rural areas. Of those who enroll, 30% are limited in their English language proficiency and about 7% are handicapped and/or institutionalized (Pugsley, 1990).

Implications

Clearly, sociodemographic variables distinguish low literate students from the general adult population. Low literates tend to be less affluent, to be more frequently unemployed and underemployed, and to have attained less schooling. Together these factors describe social and economic disadvantage and, while not all low literates are "disadvantaged," the great majority are. This has at least two implications for adult literacy education. First, it has been shown that low socioeconomic status, particularly the educational attainment component, negatively influences participation in adult education. This poses a dilemma; the segment of the adult population that needs adult literacy education the most is the least likely to seek it and to persist. As a result, student recruitment is a constant problem for most adult literacy programs and teachers must contend with dropout rates which vary from one third (Beder and Valentine, 1897) to one half (Development Associates, 1980).

Second, the low socioeconomic status of low literate adults provides a justification for the program, the justification of social and economic opportunity. It is assumed that lack of literacy constrains adults from moving up the socioeconomic ladder and that if adult literacy education is provided, low literates will avail themselves of it, thereby improving their social and economic positions. As we will see in subsequent chapters, however, the economic opportunity justification may be fallacious on several counts. First, although some adults may indeed improve their positions in society by becoming literate, it is questionable whether the total number of disadvantaged adults is significantly affected. For example, although participation in the federal program increased 48% between 1979 and 1988 (Pugsley, 1990), in the 1980s the incomes of the least affluent 20% of society decreased by $576 to a paltry $8,880 (Friedrich, 1990). Clearly, political and economic factors affect social disadvantage much more than the mere provision of educational opportunity through adult literacy education. Second, in order to have a social impact, the program must reach those who need it. On some counts success has been laudable. The program is reaching minorities, the unemployed, and the poor. Yet despite its successes, the federal ABE program still only reaches 8% of the target population (Pugsley, 1990). To fulfill its promise of social impact, the program will obviously have to reach many more of those who could benefit from it.

PSYCHOSOCIAL FACTORS

Self-Concept

The literature of adult education is replete with references regarding the importance of self-concept to participation in adult education and to successful learning (Boshier, 1973; Knox, 1977; Darkenwald & Merriam, 1982). In fact, Cross (1981) claims that self-esteem is a "kingpin" of psychological theories of motivation. Stated simply, it is claimed that adults with low self-concepts do not believe that they can be successful learners, and these beliefs become self-fulfilling. To what extent are poor self-concepts associated with low literacy? The answer is complex.

There is a great deal of evidence which suggests adult literacy professionals *believe* their students have poor self-concepts, irrespective perhaps, of whether students actually do. Fingeret (1984) notes, "Many authors cite the fact that illiterate adults bring a wealth of experience and a fully developed language system to the teaching-learning interaction; however, fear of failure, low self-esteem and self-confidence, resistance to change and a lack of future orientation, inarticulateness, fatalism, inability to cope or think abstractly, and apathy of illiterate adults are mentioned much more often" (p. 13). In a North Carolina study, Fingeret (1985) found that teachers believed that students' low self-concepts stemmed from an assumption that students had lived lives of constant failure. According to this study, the net result was a condescending attitude of teachers towards their students. James (1990) likewise notes that low self-concepts are assumed for low literacy adults and that literacy professionals believe that self-concepts must be enhanced if learners are to adapt to mainstream society. This, according to James, requires "that students become objects of assistance by providers. 'Assistentialism' is contrary to the principles of self-determination" (p. 24).

In a survey administered to 551 adult literacy teachers, Mezirow, Darkenwald, and Knox (1975) found that one fifth of the white teachers believed that 75% to 100% percent of their students lacked self-confidence, and 29% believed that half to three quarters of their students lacked self-confidence. Rosenthal (1990) portrays how her perception of students' low self-confidence affects her teaching. She writes, "Since they already enter the classroom with poor self-concepts, adult literacy students' fear of failure further limits their ability to succeed. I often stop in the middle of a lesson to discuss with students how difficult it can be to believe in themselves, to believe that they *can* understand complex material if they actively apply themselves. I remind them that bursting through the brick wall of fear takes incredible motivation, desire, and perseverance, but that it is possible to set aside their fears, anxieties, and histories of failure and proceed with learning" (p. 17).

Teachers' belief that their students have poor self-concepts seems to be based on the following logic: They dropped out of school; therefore they are failures. Because they are failures, they have low self-concepts. Furthermore, the perception seems to be that poor self-concept is a generalized trait which restricts life success on a wide array of dimensions. Why do teachers believe thus? While the logic may be partially based on observation, it might also be that the belief is derived from the social stigma attached to illiterates in the United States. As Quigley (1990a) notes, this stigma, which has roots deep in our history, views illiterates as being ignorant, incompetent, and socially impotent. The stigma is evident in and buttressed by the popular media (Ehringhaus, 1990). Not only may the perceived linkage between low self-concept and failure derive from the stigma, but, worse yet, its prevalence may perpetuate that stigma.

Whether teachers' beliefs that adult literacy students possess low self-concepts are myth or reality is an important issue. Yet this issue is difficult to resolve conclusively, as there is surprisingly little empirical research that addresses it directly. In an effort to ascertain the level of self-esteem among adult literacy students, Champagne and Young (1980) administered the Tennessee-Self Concept Scale (TSCS) to 58 high school completion students who were reading above the sixth grade level. After eight weeks the same instrument was administered to 16 of the original group as a post test to determine the effect of instruction on self-esteem. The authors found that the TSCS scores of the high school equivalency students were significantly below the norms published in the TSCS manual and that, although there was a gain in self-esteem after eight weeks of instruction, the gain was not statistically significant.

In a similar study, after administering TSCS to 113 ABE students, Close (1981) also found that TSCS scores were lower than the test's published norms. However, grade level attainment was not significantly related to self-esteem score. Likewise, Clark, Smith, and Harvey (1982) administered the TSCS to 106 ABE students and 106 high school completion students. Again the scores of both groups were found to be below the test's published norms, but contrary to Close's findings, the self-esteems of lower level ABE students were found to be higher than those of the high school equivalency students. Finally, in a Florida study, Clark and Hall (1983) administered the TSCS to 106 ABE students who all were below the eighth grade reading level. Again students' scores were found to be below the test norms.

Although all the studies employing the Tennessee Self-Concept Scale show scores for adult literacy students which were below the test norms, most were conducted on small populations and none included adults who had not participated in adult literacy in their samples. Thus we do not know to what extent low self-concept deters participation, because the self-concepts of nonparticipants have not been measured. Furthermore, as Darkenwald (1986) notes, the appropriateness of the TSCS for a low literate population is questionable, and none of the studies which employed the TSCS computed the reliability of the instrument for their study populations or discussed the instrument's validity. To further confuse the picture, when Gold and Johnson (1981) administered to 132 ABE students a different self-esteem measure, the Coopersmith Self-Esteem Inventory, they found that the subjects did not score substantially below the average. Furthermore, in the Gold and Johnson study, self-esteem was not found to be related to reading, listening, or verbal language. Similarly, when using the Coopersmith Self-Esteem Inventory, Barsch (1981) found that the self-concepts of learning disabled adult literacy students were high.

The research on the self-esteem of adult literacy students may be limited to the extent that it has tended to conceive of self-esteem as a global personality trait, when as Bandura (1977) notes, self-esteem is often situation specific. Thus it is quite possible that adult literacy students do possess a certain degree of low self-esteem but only in respect to literacy education. It might also be, however, that the behavior which teachers diagnose as low self-esteem is no more than the insecurity that most adults exhibit when faced with difficult, unknown, and protracted tasks.

Although direct attempts to measure adult literacy students' self-esteem suggest that self-esteem *may* be lower than in the general population, the results are by no means conclusive. The issue of self-esteem needs elaboration, therefore, and the literature on adult literacy dropout and program outcomes permits us to do so.

It may be assumed, albeit with caution, that if self-concept negatively affects student performance in adult literacy education, those with low self-concepts would be the least likely to persist. To ascertain whether psychological variables were associated with dropout, Wilson (1980) administered the Adjective Check List (ACL) to 142 high school completion students and ten weeks later compared the scores of dropouts (N = 29) to persisters (N = 113). From the Adjective Check List, 24 submeasures were derived including a measure of self-confidence. Wilson found that although self-control, endurance, change, abasement, and deference did significantly distinguish dropouts from persisters, self-confidence did not.

Garrison's work (1985) conflicts with Wilson's findings, however. In an 1985 effort to determine which variables discriminate between adult literacy dropouts and persisters, Garrison administered a battery of instruments to 89 adult high school completion students enrolled full time in a 15 week course. Instruments included measures of aptitude (Differential Aptitude Test), classroom environment (Classroom Environment Scale: Form F), the Social Readjustment Rating Scale, a course and goal certainty questionnaire, a rating of perceived financial concern, and the Adjective Check List which, as we have noted before, contains a measure of self-esteem. The sample included 57 persisters and 29 dropouts. Clearly Garrison had a wealth of possible predictors at his disposal and when he analyzed which variables were the most powerful predictors of persistence, self-confidence was found to be highly significant.

Like direct analyses of self-concept, studies which have dealt with the relationship between self-concept and dropout are also conflicting in their results. There is, however, one line of research in adult literacy education which has been consistent in its findings regarding self-concept, the literature on program impacts.

To determine the impact of adult literacy education on Ohio residents, Boggs, Buss, and Yarnell (1979) compared a sample of former students (N315) to a sample of adults who were eligible for adult literacy but had never participated. Former students were found to be significantly more self-confident, the inference being that participation had increased self-concept. Similarly, in a national study of the impact of adult literacy education, Development Associates (1980) interviewed 1,177 participants and found that an improvement in self-concept was the most frequently perceived outcome, reported by 84% of the respondents. In a New Jersey impact study, Valentine and Darkenwald (1986) achieved similar results with 94% of the students reporting increases in self-confidence. Impact studies in Iowa (Beder & Valentine, 1987) and in Maryland (Walker, Ewert, & Waples, 1981) have reported similar findings.

In summary, do adult literacy students have poor self concepts? Clearly many adult literacy professionals believe they do and several studies which measure adult literacy students' self-esteem with the Tennessee Self-Concept Scale show results which are below the national norm. Yet the TSCS may be an inappropriate instrument for use with adult literacy students, and research employing different measures of self-esteem produce average self-esteem scores for adult literacy students. There is research which shows that self-concept is associated with dropout, and there is research which indicates that it is not. The one set of findings which is consistent pertains to the outcomes of adult literacy education, and it seems clear that students believe that the program enhances their self-esteems. Yet positive gains in self-esteem neither prove nor disprove the contention that the self-esteems of low literate adults are lower than those of the general population. Thus in regard to the centrality of self-concept for defining the adult literacy target population, the jury is still out.

Attitudes Toward Education

From the early work of Miller (1967) to the present, the attitudes of the disadvantaged toward education have been consistently portrayed as being negative, indeed hostile. Darkenwald and Merriam (1982), for example, claim that the disadvantaged question the utility and pleasurability of education and perceive it as having little intrinsic value. Furthermore, the disadvantaged consider education to be burdensome and frightening rather than enjoyable or stimulating. Fingeret (1983, 1984) notes that adult literacy teachers locate the reasons for such attitudes in their students' past educational failures.

The available research, although sketchy, corroborates such perceptions by and large. Hayes (1988) found that of 26 reasons why adult literacy students elect not to participate, four of the five most highly ranked reasons pertained to negative attitudes:

- I thought starting classes would be difficult, with lots of questions and forms to fill out.

- I was afraid that I wasn't smart enough to do the work.

- I thought it would take me too long to finish.

- It was more important to get a job than to go to school.

Beder (1989a) notes that of 32 reasons for not participating, five of the six most highly ranked reasons pertained to negative attitudes:

- I would feel strange going back to school.

- There aren't many people in adult high school classes who are my age.

- Going back to high school would be like going to high school all over again.

- I am too old to go back to school.

- A high school diploma would not improve my life.

Kreitlow, Glustrum, and Martin (1981) found that 43% of those who had not considered obtaining a high school diploma perceived no value in acquiring the credential.

If low literate adults' attitudes toward education are negative, the object of negativity becomes an important issue. Do negative attitudes pertain to learning in general or are they related specifically to schooling—or both? Russ-Eft and McLaughlin (1981) shed light on the issue. They report that while 67% of adults with less than high school in age groups 30, 50, and 70 rated the importance of learning and education to be very or moderately important, 91% of those with some post secondary schooling rated education and learning to be moderately or very important. Thus although more highly educated adults seem to place greater value on education, there are still sizeable numbers of poorly educated adults who place considerable value on education. While Russ-Eft and McLaughlin measured attitudes toward education in general, the Hayes, Beder, and Kreitlow et al. studies all measured attitudes specifically concerning adult literacy education. The consensus of these studies seems to be that negative attitudes pertain to schooling itself, rather than to learning.

There are two possible explanations for negative attitudes toward education which we will discuss in detail in subsequent chapters. The first is that the low value placed on education is a class trait which is learned through childhood socialization. Lower class adults simply value doing over intellectual pursuits. Most studies show that the most common reason for leaving school is the desire to work. For lower class adults, work may simply be a more meaningful life pursuit that studying. The second explanation, which seems to be part of the belief systems of many adult literacy professionals, is that previous schooling for low literacy adults was fraught with failure and anguish. Thus negative attitudes are formed through direct experience with the public school system, an experience which was unpleasant and entailed few rewards.

The Deficit Model

The evidence shows that the adult literacy target population is less affluent, is more educationally disadvantaged, and has a higher proportion of minorities. Low literate students have negative attitudes toward education and schooling and adult literacy professionals believe that their students lack self-confidence, although there is no conclusive evidence that they do. This profile forms the backdrop for what Fingeret (1984) terms the deficit model of adult literacy education. Adult literacy students are perceived as being fragile and afflicted with deficits which need treatment, rehabilitation, and remediation. It is believed that only through rehabilitation will the low literate be able to fit into mainstream society. But does a deficit model necessarily follow from the profile of adult low literates presented here? Probably not, and there is an alternative.

To a large extent the deficit model stems from a clash of subcultures. Those of the dominant subculture, "middle class

America," perceive the lower class subculture as being lacking and
in need of major mending. This perception, however, ignores the
fact that subcultures are the way they are because they have adapted
to both the material conditions with which they are presented and
to the dominant ideologies and value systems of the social order. It
is important, for example, to have a subculture which values doing
over thinking for without it the dominant society can not be guar-
anteed an ample supply of manual labor. The alternative to the deficit model then is a model which locates itself in the low literate
subculture rather than in middle class culture, a model which focuses on helping low literates to understand the meanings which
constitute *their* world and, in doing so, enables them to control it.
In such a model, akin to Freire and Macedo's (1987) emancipatory
education and Fingeret and Jurmo's (1989) participatory literacy
education, "ownership" of the programs rests with the learners, and
teachers educate *with* rather than educating *on*.

CHAPTER 3

Learners' Motivation

Learners' motivations for participation are central to understanding adult literacy, for while children have to attend school, adults participate in literacy programs because they choose to. Motivation is the force which impels voluntary adult learners toward literacy education. When it is strong, adults can be expected to overcome the barriers to participation that life imposes. When motivation is weak, participation is highly unlikely. It follows that if literacy programs can develop recruitment and instruction which is congruent with learners' motivations, success in attracting and retaining students will be considerably enhanced.

An understanding of motivation is necessary at the policy level as well as at the local program level. Public funds are allocated to adult literacy education primarily because of its social benefits, benefits which accrue to society as a whole as well as to those who are educated. Yet the fact that society recognizes the importance of literacy is no guarantee that learners will be motivated to expend their time and effort in achieving it. If learners are to participate and society is to reap the benefits, policy must also take learners' motivation into account.

Our discussion of motivation has two dimensions. It will begin with a general discussion of motivation and draw implications for adult literacy. Relevant here are theoretical models derived from psychology, socialization theory, marketing theory, and critical pedagogy as well as research which is primarily descriptive in nature. Subsequently, the discussion will move to work which is specific to the adult literacy population.

GENERAL THEORY AND RESEARCH

Psychological Models

The common element of psychological models is a focus on motivation as an individual trait, although most models recognize that individual motivation is at least in part influenced by the environment. Motivational models of participation go back at least twenty years. Since many of the concepts incorporated in these models have lasting significance, it is useful to examine psychological models in historical context.

Force Field Analysis

The first model of note is Miller's (1967) Force Field Analysis. Miller begins with a simple premise: Learners participate in adult education in order to satisfy needs, needs which are ordered hierarchically and are strongly influenced by social class differences. Miller's notion of needs is derived from Maslow's needs hierarchy, and his concept of class is based on the work of Gans (1962). Following Maslow, Miller theorizes that before learners can seek to fulfill higher order needs, they must first satisfy basic needs, the most basic of which is the need for survival: food, shelter, and the like. After survival comes safety, the basic need for security. Then comes belonging, "the deep emotional needs we seek to satisfy in marriage to the pervasive needs for acceptance by the members of whatever groups are important to us" (p. 5).

The hierarchy moves on to a series of ego needs which Miller believes are the most fundamental and do not become powerful motivators until the basic needs of survival, safety, and belonging have been met. These higher order needs include recognition and achievement, which Miller equates with a need to achieve social status, and finally self-realization (often termed self-actualization).

There is nothing unique in Miller's use of Maslow to explain motivation to participate in adult education. This was a popular convention in the late 1960s and early 1970s (Knowles, 1970; Kidd, 1973). However, Miller's superimposition of social class on motivation separates his work from others. Miller divides class into five categories: Lower-lower, working class, lower middle, upper middle, and upper class.

Regarding the lower-lower class, Miller states: "The lower-

lowers, who are the primary target of the current anti-poverty programs, are the only group which is actually hostile to education, because it conflicts with basic life values arising out of their class position at the bottom on the heap. An unstable work and family life encourages an action—and excitement—orientation, a belief in luck and fate, and absorption in the immediate present. To all these values, education is inimical because it requires a strong enough belief in a future payoff to give up present gratifications" (p. 9). Lower-lowers, then, are at the bottom of the needs hierarchy, and their value system makes participation problematic.

Although Miller views working class youth as being action-oriented, as working class youths age they become "absorbed into the routine-seeking peer group culture . . . in which the dominant values are economic security and group loyalty" (p. 9). Although the payoff of education does not have to be immediate for working class learners, there does need to be a practical reward if they are to participate. The working class, then, is dominated by needs for safety and belonging.

Working class adults perceive life in terms of "them against us" and reject middle class orientations toward abstractions such as career, justice, truth, and community. These abstract orientations which characterize the middle class operate at the higher end of the needs hierarchy. Lower middle class learners are motivated by a desire to increase their social status, and among upper middle class learners "There is a devotion to career advancement that transcends an interest in status for status' sake; a great concern for self-development that separates self from the family unit; and a cosmopolitanism that directs attention away from community and local associational concerns to national and international ones" (p. 12).

Miller concludes his model by weaving the threads of needs hierarchy and social class orientation into a tapestry of force field analysis based on Lewin's work. He weighs the positive and negative influences on participation in four areas: education for vocational competence, for personal and family competence, for citizenship competence, and for self-development; the general conclusion is that participation is more likely as social class status increases.

What does Miller's model of motivation mean for adult literacy education? There are two implications. First, Miller associates motivation with social class values claiming that lower and working class values are inimical to participation. If it is assumed that the majority of low literates come from the lower and working class, then we are left with a significant problem: to increase participation in adult literacy education the class value structure must be changed, and this would require a massive social intervention well beyond the scope of the publicly funded adult literacy system.

Yet Miller may be guilty of the logic of social determinism. Society produces a class structure; the class structure creates a value system hostile to adult education; lower classes are not motivated to participate; there is nothing we can realistically do. As Giroux (1983) notes, however, such a logic leaves no place for human agency—the possibility that, through collective action, the lower classes can transform the social structures that reproduce the class structure. Indeed this is the very objective of those adult literacy programs which employ an emancipatory education model. Nevertheless, in drawing the relationship between class values and participation, Miller may be making an important point: Although adult literacy programs which define their purpose as helping individuals to rise in the social system may have some success, the mere provision of educational opportunity may do little to alter the class structures which foster adult illiteracy in the first place.

Second, Miller claims that the needs of low literate adults are influenced by a needs hierarchy. They are motivated by basic needs for survival rather than by higher order needs such as recognition and self-actualization. If they participate at all, their reasons for doing so are limited to needs for the basics—food, shelter, and money. As we will discuss later in this chapter, there is no empirical basis for this assumption.

A Congruence Model

The congruence model of motivation to participate in adult education is associated with the work of Boshier (1973, 1977). Based on a factor analysis of 48 motives for attendance, Boshier noted two basic underlying motivations which he labeled deficiency and growth. Growth oriented learners are expressing rather than coping; they are intrinsically motivated by internal factors. In contrast, deficiency oriented learners are "impelled by social and environmental pressures" (Boshier, 1973, p. 256). Like Miller, Boshier makes reference to Maslow, theorizing that deficiency oriented learners are motivated to meet lower order needs, while self actualizing, growth oriented learners seek to meet higher order needs. "In growth-oriented people the ordinary or conventional dichotomy between work and play is transcended, whereas the deficiency-oriented person regards both education and work as something separate from the rest of his life" (Boshier, 1973, p. 258).

Again following Maslow, Boshier theorizes that deficiency oriented learners are characterized by intra-self (self/ideal) incongruence. That is to say that there is a disparity between how they "define" themselves and how they want to be.

Intra-self incongruence leads to self/other incongruence, a disparity between how learners perceive themselves and how they perceive others, such as teachers and other students, reacting to them. In turn, incongruences lead to anxiety which in turn causes learners to avoid participation.

Growth oriented learners are characterized by correspondence between their actual selves (how they define themselves to be), their ideal selves (whom they aspire to be), and others (how they expect others to react to themselves). Freed from the anxiety associated with incongruence, these "fully functioning" learners are open to new experiences and are likely to participate and to persist.

Boshier believes that incongruences are mediated by age in that the process of becoming adult entails incongruences which are ameliorated by later growth and maturity. Hence, younger adults tend to be more deficiency motivated than older adults and are less likely to participate and persist. Boshier claims that a test of the theory on a sample of 233 adults generally supports congruence theory.

Although Boshier does not state it directly, he implies that many low literates are deficiency oriented and have not satisfied the lower order needs in Maslow's hierarchy. The deficiency oriented lack intrinsic motivation, have deterministic attitudes, are fearful of the environment, and "possess attitudes which cluster around money, basic need-gratifications (rather than 'growth' values), sheer habits, stimulus binding, neurotic needs, convention and inertia and . . . doing what other people expect and demand" (p. 258).

How many low literates are deficiency oriented? We do not know, but the psychological profile which Boshier presents is hardly optimistic in respect to their participation in adult literacy education. It has always been assumed that low literate adults participate in literacy education because they are motivated to improve themselves. Yet according to Boshier deficiency oriented adults are not so motivated. In fact, they are hardly motivated to participate in adult education at all.

Both Boshier and Miller suggest a similar vision of the low literate population, especially those who are not inclined to seek literacy education. For both, the low literate population is riddled with deficits, deficits which must be corrected if participation is to be expected and learning is to take place. Such a vision obviously supports the deficit model of adult literacy education which assumes that low literates are poorly educated and unsuccessful because of psychological and social problems that have constrained their social mobility. These assumptions support a teaching-learning technology of adult literacy education based on the "medical model." The process begins with diagnosis of individual deficits and moves to the prescription of a personal treatment. When the treatment is complete, students are expected to be socially and educationally "well." There may be two problems with such thinking, however. First, defining adult low literates as deficit ridden supports and perpetuates the very social stigma attached to low literacy which limits life success and reduces motivation. Second, a focus on individual deficit may disembed low literacy from its sociocultural context. It ignores the possibility that low literacy, and the problems associated with it, is a social construction which can only be ameliorated through social change.

Expectancy-Valence

The expectancy-valence model of motivation to participate is closely associated with Rubenson (1977), although its roots go back to the work of Vroom (1964) and Porter and Lawler (1968). While Miller and Boshier's models of general motivation to participate might be criticized for their oversimplification, expectancy-valence theory tends to err toward complexity.

For Rubenson, motivation to participate is based on two components: expectancy and valence. Expectancy pertains to learners' perceptions that participation will be successful and outcomes will be positive. For expectancy to be positive, learners must believe that they "can do it" and that the results of learning will be beneficial. If either component of expectancy is zero, there is no motivation to participate. One's expectancy is based primarily on previous experience and on the perception and interpretation of the environment.

Valence, which refers to the magnitude of values ascribed to the consequences of participation, can be positive, indifferent, or negative. Learners weigh the consequences of participating according to their current needs. Thus, in examining the consequences of participation, an adult literacy student might reason, "yes, on one hand I will learn to read and I will feel better about myself, but no, I can not afford the time away from my family." Valence represents the sum total of such deliberations. Taken together, expectancy and valence determine the force of motivation and hence whether an individual is likely to participate.

Although Rubenson's model is largely untested, there are two recent works which have utilized components of the expectancy-valence model. Van Tilberg and Dubois (1989) studied barriers and encouragers to participation, as derived conceptually from Vroom's model of expectancy-valence. Their study population included 29 ABE/GED students in Columbus, Ohio, and 29 students enrolled in any of four programs leading to certification examinations in London, England. Barriers to participation were found to include embarrassment, low anticipation of success, and previous negative educational experiences. Encouragers to participation included needing education for a job, desiring self-improvement, feeling concern for children, and avoiding current conditions.

In 1988 Joseph studied the relationship between components of Porter and Lawler's (1968) expectancy-valence model and participation of managers in job related continuing education. The components of the model selected were the perceived value of rewards for participating, the perceived amount of effort required to participate, and the perceived abilities required to participate successfully. Following Porter and Lawler, it was postulated that motivation to participate would be enhanced when perceived value was high, when the perceived effort required was low, and when potential learners perceived that they possessed the abilities required of the learning. When elements of the three variables were regressed on various measures of participation, however, none explained enough of the variance to support a conclusion that the model was effective in predicting participation.

In its basic form, an expectancy-valence model of motivation in adult literacy education would have to consider potential learners' expectancy that participation will be successful and the perceived consequences (valence) of participation. Participation in adult literacy education is not easy. It is protracted in duration; the possibility that life problems will interfere is high, and some low literates may fear failure. Thus it may be that motivation to participate is sapped by a low expectation of success. It may also be that the perceived consequences of participating do not entail sufficient reward for many. After all, there are other ways to cope with low literacy which do not require the effort of learning to read and write.

Chain of Response

Making reference to Miller, Boshier, and Rubenson, Cross (1981) developed a chain of response model (COR) which "assumes that participation in a learning activity, whether organized in classes or self-directed, is not a single act but the result of a chain of responses, each based on an evaluation of the position of the individual in his or her environment" (p. 125).

The chain begins with self-evaluation which is highly related to self-confidence. As Cross states, "persons who lack confidence in their own abilities . . . avoid putting themselves to the test and are unlikely to volunteer for learning" (p. 125). Attitudes toward adult education, which can be positive, negative, or indifferent, are the second link of the chain.

The third link recognizes the importance of goals and is for the most part derived from expectancy valence theory. This link has two components: the importance of the goal to the learner and the learner's belief about whether obtaining the goal will lead to reward. Whether a learner expects to be successful is, like attitudes about education, related to self-esteem "in that individuals with high self-esteem 'expect' to be successful, whereas those with less self-confidence entertain doubts" (p. 126).

Goals are influenced by life transitions, such as changing employment or the birth of a child, which trigger goal formation. Motivation alone, however, is insufficient to yield participation as there must also be educational opportunities and a lack of significant barriers, both of which are influenced by the information available about adult education. When the elements in the model are positive, participation is likely; successful participation feeds back into the system enhancing future motivation and, hence, the likelihood of continued participation.

The chain of response model is holistic, attempting to account for as many factors associated with motivation as possible. Although unlike the models of Miller and Boshier it does not postulate a hierarchy of needs, it does make central use of the concept "self-esteem," as do Miller, Boshier, Rubenson, and many others.

As discussed in the preceding chapter, adult literacy teachers generally believe that the self-esteem of their students is low and is rooted in previous failure. While the empirical evidence neither confirms or refutes this belief, it is clear that teachers place a great deal of emphasis on addressing learners' self-esteem. One strategy for doing so is the purposeful development of self-esteem by minimizing failure, providing emotional support, and lauding success, however minimal. As Fingeret (1985) and Mezirow, Darkenwald, and Knox (1975) note, this is the norm. Yet such a stance toward adult literacy students may lead to a patronizing, condescending attitude which treats adult learners as children. The other option is to acknowledge that low self-esteem is more of a social construction than a psychological trait. If low literate adults have low self-esteem, it is because they have internalized the perceptions of failure that the dominant society has of them. The goal in this case is to assist low literate adults to understand the reasons for their low self-esteem and, in doing so, to free them from it.

Socialization and Life Cycle Factors

Theorists of socialization and those who study the adult life cycle conclude that motivation to learn is produced by a need to solve the problems that adult life poses. For example, in a study of nearly 2,000 adults age 25 or older, Aslanian and Brickell (1980) found that 83% of those studied were motivated to learn by a past, present, or future change in their lives, and 56% mentioned a career transition as a motivation to learn. Futhermore, all who claimed that a life transition motivated their learning could identify a specific "trigger event" that initiated the learning activity. While Aslanian and Brickell's research has been criticized for its methodological flaws, the notion that motivation is produced by a need to resolve life posed problems is supported by a wealth of literature in adult education (Knowles, 1980; Knox, 1977; Tough, 1982; Boucouvalas & Krupp, 1989).

The process through which life events trigger motivation to learn is informed by socialization theory, and this is aptly delineated by Mortimer and Simmons (1978). Socialization is the process

through which individuals learn the behaviors and attitudes necessary for functioning in society. While socialization occurs throughout life, it is qualitatively different during adulthood in terms of the
content, context, and response to socialization.

In respect to content, "childhood is thought to be concerned
with the regulation of biological drives; in adolescence, with the
development of overarching values and the self-image; while in
adulthood socialization is seen by many as involving more overt and
specific norms and behaviors (such as those related to the work
role), as well as more superficial personality features. . . . Adult socialization is more realistic, involving the synthesis of what has been
learned previously and the development of modes of reconciling
contradictory normative standards" (p. 423). Thus while preadult
socialization entails learning content which prepares the individual
for life, adult socialization includes all the fine adjustments needed
for living one's life. Although individuals, for example, may learn
the basic values of industry and time organization necessary for
work roles during their preadult years, what workers actually do
can not be learned until they take on these roles in adulthood.

Thus it is evident that adult socialization is different from
childhood socialization and that the problems posed by adult socialization create motivation to participate in adult literacy education; recognition of these factors highlights the adultness of adult
literacy education. For adults, motivation is derived from the need
to perform in a specific life context such as parent or worker. While
for preadults literacy may be an artificially induced end in itself, for
adults the motivation to acquire literacy is derived from the need to
perform basic life roles more effectively. Thus while for preadults
the basic motivation to learn to read and write may be based in
compliance with authority, for adults motivation to become literate
is based in the enabling capacity of literacy. It follows that adults
who believe in the enabling capacity of literacy are likely to participate while those who do not, are not.

In respect to the context of socialization, Mortimer and Simmons cite research which suggests that while preadults are socialized
by the family, school, and peer group where "Relationships between
the socializees and socializers (parents, friends, teachers) are likely
to be more affectively charged than in later periods" (p. 424), adult
socialization is characterized by more formal experiences with such

persons as superiors, co-workers, and clients. Childhood socialization is basically anticipatory, and the institutions which socialize
also nurture. Adult socialization, in contrast, takes place in the real
world where the consequences of poor role performance have direct
and immediate consequences. Motivation to participate in adult
education is linked, therefore, to direct and immediate application,
a conclusion which Knowles (1970, 1980) also reaches, albeit from
a different direction. Given this, it is quite possible that there are
discontinuities between school based adult literacy models that are
implicitly oriented to the future application orientations of preadults, and adult clients, who are orientated toward immediate, real
world application.

In terms of response to socialization, Mortimer and Simmons
note that preadults may be more "malleable" than adults, since by
the time individuals reach adulthood they have already been subjected to a considerable amount of socialization and are thus more
resistant to change. Yet much adult socialization is voluntary, and
adults have a much greater choice in how they are socialized. They
are able to avoid socializing experiences which they find to be
uncomfortable and are able to seek out experiences which they consider to be rewarding. This points to the critical relationship between previous school experience and adults' motivation to pursue
literacy education. In cases where the socialization experience in
elementary and secondary schooling was unpleasant and conflict
ridden, adults' negative attitudes and lack of motivation toward
schooling are likely to be difficult to change. At the same time, as
adults, low literates are free to avoid school, and unfortunately often
do.

The need to learn new behaviors and attitudes during adulthood, and the motivation to learn which has been triggered by that
need are derived from at least two sources of change: the life cycle
and social change itself. In respect to the life cycle, it is important
to note that the full content of most adult roles is relatively invisible
to individuals who have not obtained full incumbency in the role
and is thus impossible to master adequately through anticipatory
socialization. One can not fully appreciate what it is to be a spouse
or parent until one actually becomes one, nor can one deal with the
hidden norms of the workplace until those norms are encountered.
Hence, as adults move through the life cycle, new motivations to

learn are constantly being generated by the need to perform new roles. Thus adults' motivations to pursue adult literacy are likely to vary over time, and the magnitude of motivation is likely to wax and to wane.

An equally powerful source of the need for adult socialization is social change itself. Social norms change, and so must adult behaviors and attitudes. Rachal (1990), for example, portrays dynamic social change for adult education in demography, the workplace, and social norms. Indeed, the impact of social change on adult motivation to learn has been a recurrent theme in adult education since the 1920s (Beder, 1989b). Rapid change in the workplace, for example, has resulted in a tremendous social press for employee resocialization and increased literacy. Although education and, unfortunately, workers are often blamed, a great deal of the need for workplace literacy derives simply from the fact that more sophisticated literacy skills are required as time passes.

While the need to perform adult roles creates motivation to learn, the multiplicity of roles adults must perform also creates deterrents to learning. While deterrents will be considered in more detail in a subsequent chapter, it is important to note here that role multiplicity often produces role conflict—a need to perform role behaviors which are incompatible. For example, what happens when an adult literacy student, who is also a mother, is faced with the alternative of attending class, an expectation of the student role, and caring for a sick child, something that mothers *must* do? Such conflicts are not always resolved in favor of the student role, nor should they be, and the tension that results from conflicting motivations can be difficult indeed for the individual.

Socialization theory then views motivation to learn as being a product of the socially imposed need for adults to master the behaviors and attitudes required of adult roles, roles which constantly change throughout the life cycle in a dynamic society. In this tradition, motivation is less a product of individual psychological traits and more a product of the requirements of social living. While motivation can be studied from the perspective of how individuals negotiate socially imposed needs, it can also be studied from the perspective of how social institutions, such as the family or workplace, create needs and how institutional environments, the adult literacy classroom for example, facilitate or impede learning.

Motivation as Demand

While psychological models have tended to view motivation as an individual trait and socialization theory considers it to be a socially induced phenomenon, the concept of demand, a concept which is derived from marketing theory, looks at motivation from a economic perspective. Demand is defined as the degree to which an individual actually wants to participate in adult education, thus recognizing that while there may be large numbers of adults who *need* adult literacy according to society's definition of need, the proportion of adults who exhibit a demand for it may be much smaller. This smaller number has often been referred to as "the demand population" for ABE (Development Associates, 1980).

Kotler (1975) notes several levels of demand. In "negative demand" potential learners actually avoid participation. It is not known for what proportion of the adult literacy population demand is negative, but work by Beder and Quigley (1990) suggests that the proportion may be substantial. When faced with negative demand, the object is to convert the negative market, "to analyze the sources of the market's resistance; whether they lie largely in the area of *beliefs* about the offering, in the *values* touched upon by the offering, in the raw *feelings* engendered by the offering, or in the *cost* of acquiring the offering" (Kotler, p. 82). Once the source of resistance has been determined, the objective is to change it. Unfortunately, this is generally extremely difficult to do (Beder, 1980).

The second level of demand is "no demand" and, in this case, although potential learners do not avoid participation, neither do they seek it; they are simply indifferent. The strategy in this case is to motivate the market through stimulational advertising, to connect education to something which is valued by the market (job acquisition for example), or to alter the environment to make the learning more attractive. Moving the location of learning to a more attractive setting might be an example of environmental alteration.

The third demand state is "latent demand." In this case potential learners want an educational offering which does not exist and the object is quite simple. To be successful, the educator needs only to identify the demand and create the offering to meet it (Beder, 1986).

Fundamental to an understanding of motivation "as demand"

is the understanding of the mechanism which produces that demand—or the lack of it. That basic mechanism is the concept of
exchange (Kotler, 1975; Beder, 1980, 1986). Low literates will participate if, and only if, they expect to gain more from participation
than the value of what they must give up. That is to say, in participating learners exchange valued resources, such as time and money,
for something they value more. Unless the exchange is positive for
the learner, there will be no participation.

Critical to an understanding of the exchange relationship is a
knowledge of the essential benefit potential learners seek in the
exchange, and this is not always obvious. For example, while adult
literacy students may say that they have enrolled to earn a GED
diploma, for many the essential benefit may be desire for general
self-improvement or to meet family responsibilities (Beder & Valentine, 1987).

Conceiving motivation as demand recognizes that perceived
need alone is insufficient to produce participation. Indeed, for demand for adult literacy to be positive, not only must potential learners "perceive" the need, but they must also *want* the education,
believe that the provider can effectively supply it, and *prefer* the offering to any of its competitors (Beder, 1990). Thus the demand concept recognizes that motivation results not only from basic needs,
but, in fact, from the interaction between needs and the object of
their fulfillment—whatever adult literacy offerings are available.

Framing the concept of motivation in the rubric of marketing
theory may have a practical implication: While other models of motivation may be useful in helping us to understand motivation, and
perhaps even in predicting participation, they lack practical prescriptions for doing much about it. On the other hand, not only is
the demand concept based on a theoretical foundation, but it also
includes proven techniques for application (Beder, 1986).

Critical Pedagogy

Although critical pedagogy, which is associated with such
thinkers as Paulo Freire, Henry Giroux, Stanley Aronowitz, and others, does not focus specifically on motivation in the context of a
theoretical model, it does entail a powerful critique of the manner
in which motivation has been generally conceived. For critical ped-

agogues, motivation and the lack of it is culturally configured. If the poor and oppressed lack motivation to participate in adult education, it is not because they are somehow deficient, but because an unequal society has suppressed and depressed their motivation through the cultural processes which reproduce society.

Freire (1970) notes that the oppressors of society cause the oppressed to believe that they are deficient, because such belief systems disempower the oppressed and block their motivation to challenge the unequal social order. This is manifest in self-depreciation, which is another way of defining a low self-concept. Freire notes, "Self-depreciation is another characteristic of the oppressed, which derives from their internalization of the opinion the oppressors hold of them. So often do they hear that they are good for nothing, know nothing, and are incapable of learning anything—that they are sick, lazy, and unproductive—that in the end they become convinced of their own unfitness" (Freire, 1970, p. 49).

Giroux and Aronowitz (1985) focus on the public schools as institutions which "reproduce" an unequal social order, institutions which produce motivation for further education in some and suppress it in others. They state, "Contrary to the claims of liberal theorists and historians that public education offers possibilities for individual development, social mobility, and political and economic power to the disadvantaged and dispossessed, radical educators have argued that the main functions of schools are the reproduction of the dominant ideology, its forms of knowledge, and the distribution of skills needed to reproduce the social division of labor" (p. 69).

According to Quigley (1990b), many underclass youths come into conflict with the school system values that function as reproduction mechanisms and they resist. These "resisters" then drop out and avoid any further school oriented efforts to educate them, efforts such as adult literacy education. Resistance is considered to be almost a virtue, a rational response to an intolerable situation.

In the tradition of critical pedagogy, motivation to participate in adult education may be conceived as "cultural capital," a term coined by Bordieu and Passeron (1977). Cultural capital, like economic capital, is distributed unequally by a society which seeks to maintain its class oriented social structure. Through the various institutions of society, particularly the schools, higher class youths obtain more cultural capital, such as socially valued speech patterns, while lower class youths receive less. This puts higher class youths at a distinct advantage as they achieve adulthood, because they have more cultural capital to "invest" in their own behalf.

From the perspective of critical pedagogy then, motivation may be conceived as a class trait. The cultural mechanisms of an unequal society instill motivation for continued education in some while suppressing it in others as part of the social reproduction process. Society needs an underclass to do the kinds of work only an underclass will do. In this scheme low literacy and the perpetuation of it has a distinct place. By suppressing the motivation of the underclasses to become literate, the advantaged classes secure their position in the social order and maintain their dominance.

Descriptive Research

Up to this point this chapter has considered theoretical models of motivation, models which are designed to explain and predict. Another tradition of motivation research, however, has primarily focused on describing what the motivators are.

Much of this descriptive work owes its genesis to the work of Houle (1961). Based on a relatively small number of personal interviews (N = 22) of a nonrepresentative sample, Houle postulated that there were three basic motivational orientations: the goal oriented, the activity oriented, and the learning oriented.

Goal oriented learners are motivated to achieve a specific outcome. In Houle's words, for goal oriented learners "knowledge is to be put to use, and, if it is not, why bother to pursue it?" (p. 16). Activity oriented learners are motivated "for reasons unrelated to the purposes or content of the activities in which they engage" (p. 19) such as to dispel loneliness or to meet other people; learning oriented learners are motivated to learn for the sake of learning itself.

Guided by Houle's provocative work, Boshier (1971) developed the 48 item Educational Participation Scale. When the items of the scale were factor analyzed with a large sample of New Zealand adults, as reported earlier, Boshier found two basic motivational orientations which he termed deficiency oriented and growth oriented. In 1974 Morstain and Smart replicated Boshier's work on a U.S. sample and found six basic motivational orientations: desire to improve "Social Relationships," desire to fulfill "External Expectations," motivation to promote "Social Welfare," desire to attain "Professional Advancement," need for "Escape Stimulation," and motivation for "Cognitive Interest."

Following Boshier's development of the Educational Participation Scale, there were many replications of the factor analytic approach to motivational orientation research which utilized his instrumentation. Employing a Canadian sample, Boshier (1977) himself found five factors, or basic motivational orientations: Escape Stimulation, Professional Advancement, Social Welfare, External Expectations, and Cognitive Interest. In reviewing 15 years of motivational orientation research, Boshier (1976) concluded that while there were some differences in factor structure across studies, "the orientations are reasonably stable across time and space" (p. 44). Finally, in what Boshier and Collins (1985) called a "large scale empirical test," a design which used data from numerous studies and employed cluster analysis rather than factor analysis, the authors moved full circle, claiming that Houle was basically correct, that "the goal and learning orientations were reasonably clear as Houle had described them, but the activity orientation was much more complex than he had envisaged; a forced aggregate of Social Stimulation, Social Contact, External Expectations and Community Service items" (p. 128).

The motivational orientation research has been conducted on a multiplicity of populations in many different contexts. Since the findings seem to hold up well, it is reasonable to assume that the same motivational orientations roughly apply to low literate adults —that low literate adults are motivated by some configuration of response to the following factors: escape stimulation, professional advancement, social welfare, external expectations, and cognitive interest. Yet for two reasons generalization to the low literate population may be inappropriate. First, if the psychological motivation models of Miller and Boshier hold true, low literate adults behave very differently from more advantaged adults in respect to motivation. Second, most of the motivation orientation literature pertains to a motivation to attend short courses. It may be that the protracted nature of adult literacy education significantly affects learners' motivation to enroll in it.

Another tradition of descriptive research was initiated by Johnstone and Rivera (1965) in one of the most comprehensive studies of participation in adult education ever conducted. Beginning with

a probability sample of 13,293 U.S. households, the researchers
were successful in contacting 90% (N = 11,957). Johnstone and Rivera (p. 143) queried their respondents who had taken adult education courses (N = 4,603) about their reasons for doing so. They
found that the three most important reasons were "to become a
better person" (37%), to "prepare for a new job or promotion"
(36%), and to obtain help "on the job I held at the time" (32%).
Other reasons listed included to "spend my spare time more enjoy-
ably (20%), to "meet new and interesting people" (15%), to carry
out "everyday tasks and duties around home" (13%), "to get away
from the daily routine" (10%), and to carry out "everyday tasks
and duties away from home" (10%).

This data led Johnstone and Rivera to conclude that vocational
reasons for participating were extremely important. When the vocational oriented reasons were analyzed according to socioeconomic
levels, the authors concluded that "men and women of lower socioeconomic status, for example, were much more likely to use adult
education for job preparation than for advancement, while the opposite was true for participants of higher socioeconomic status. In
lower social class positions, in other words, it appears that the main
function of vocational education is to place people in new jobs; at
higher levels, on the other hand, vocational education functions
much more to advance one's position on the job already held" (p.
159).

The notion that low literate adults might be primarily motivated for vocational reasons fits well with a human capital argument for adult literacy education. We fund adult literacy education
so that learners can acquire jobs or obtain better jobs; they are
motivated to do the same; all is well. Yet such a conclusion belies
the fact that, according to Johnstone and Rivera, the most important
motivation for participating is basic self-improvement and basic self-
improvement goes well beyond vocational motivation in its scope.

In 1972 Carp, Peterson, and Roelfs (Cross & Valley, 1975)
conducted another large scale study of participation in the tradition
of Johnstone and Rivera. Again employing a large probability sample (2,515 households, 2,974 individuals) to which 2,004 persons
(67%) responded, the authors divided the respondents into two
groups: "learners" who reported receiving instruction in the past
year, and "would-be learners" who reported an interest in some kind
of learning.

Both learners and would-be learners were asked to indicate the importance of 20 reasons for learning derived primarily from Burgess's (1971) work. It was found that for both learners and would-be learners "to become better informed" was the most important reason, or motivation, for learning. Thirty-five percent of the would-be learners indicated that to "satisfy curiosity" was very important, as compared to 32% of the learners, thus demonstrating that this reason was important for both groups. The authors found, however, that while to get a new job was very important to 25% of the would-be learners, it was less important to learners (18%), and that while "to advance in present job" was very important to 25% of the learners, only 17% of the would-be learners indicated it was very important.

The five most important reasons for learning among would-be learners were found to be to become better informed; to become a happier person; to satisfy curiosity; to be a better parent, spouse; and to become a better citizen. In contrast, the five most important reasons for learners were to become better informed, to satisfy curiosity, to satisfy employer, to become a happier person, and to advance in the present job.

Generally speaking, then, the work of Carp, Peterson, and Roelfs does not confirm the high vocational motivation for participation found by Johnstone and Rivera, especially among those who are defined as would-be learners. Instead, Carp, Peterson, and Roelf's research points to the importance of less instrumental motives such as acquiring general knowledge, satisfying curiosity, and becoming happier. If these same reasons apply to low literate adults, the theory that low literate adults' motivations are based on highly instrumental survival needs—a notion central to the congruency model and that of Miller—falls apart.

Reports of the National Center for Educational Statistics (NCES) represent another source of descriptive data, although NCES figures include participation in part-time credit courses taken for high school or college credit, and this may slightly distort the picture. NCES issued reports on participation in adult education every three years beginning in 1969 and ending in 1984. In summarizing trends in reasons for participating between 1969 and 1984, the NCES (Hill, 1987) states, "Many people, when they think of adult education activities, picture courses taken for general information, personal or social reasons such as buying a house, ceramics, or wine tasting. While courses taken for these reasons are a significant part of adult education, they compose about half of all adult education activities in 1969, but declined to one-third of all adult education by 1984" (p. 5). While in 1969 only half the courses taken were for job advancement reasons, in 1984 two thirds of the courses taken were for job advancement.

NCES data demonstrates that reasons for participation are gender-related. The authors note that while the increase in job related adult education prior to 1978 was due to an increase in the number of women participants, after 1978 the increase is accounted for by increased participation by both men and women. In respect to courses taken for general, personal or social purposes, "women outnumbered men 2 to 1 throughout the 15-year period under examination. In job-related courses, men outnumbered women 2 to 1 in 1969, but by 1984 men were slightly outnumbered by women" (p. 7).

NCES data suggests a strong motivation to participate for vocational reasons, although it is possible that the upward trend of participation in vocationally oriented courses is due to an increased availability of courses rather than to an increase in motivation. The data also suggests that the objects of motivation—the types of courses adults are motivated to pursue—are affected by sociodemographic variables such as gender.

MOTIVATIONS OF LOW LITERATE ADULTS

The Iowa Adult Literacy Studies

The Iowa Adult Literacy Studies (Beder & Valentine, 1987, 1990; Beder, 1989a) provide perhaps the most extensive contemporary analysis of low literate adult motivations. As previously noted, the study was conducted on a random sample of 323 Iowa ABE students who had completed less than 11 grades of schooling; one of the several objectives of the research was to determine what the basic motives for attending were.

The study began with the development of items for an interview schedule which was later administered to the sample by trained researchers in face to face interviews which lasted about one half hour. In a departure from the motivational orientation research which based item generation in previous theory, the researchers generated their items from the analysis of open ended interviews with ABE students themselves. The qualitative analysis of open ended interviews resulted in 62 motivations which were grounded in the reality of ABE. Whenever possible, items were written in the actual language of the ABE students who had voiced them.

The research subjects were then asked how true each motivation item was for them, "not true," "somewhat true," or "very true," and the responses were translated into a three point Likert scale with "not true" being set at one.

When item means were computed, it was found that the five motivations with the highest mean scores were as follows.

1. I want to learn new things (mean = 2.86)

2. I enjoy learning new things (mean = 2.85)

3. I want to get a high school diploma (mean = 2.82)

4. I want to improve myself so I can finish school (mean = 2.75)

5. I want to be more intelligent (mean = 2.71)

Interestingly, none of the vocationally related items such as "I want to get a better job" or "I need to make more money" were among the highest ranked motivations.

A simple analysis of 62 items, however, was a task of such complexity that it was difficult to draw conclusions. Consequently, the researchers sought to determine if there were an underlying structure in motivation to attend ABE—they sought a more simple and parsimonious way to conceive motivation. To do this they employed factor analysis, a statistical procedure which groups items according to the patterns in which interview subjects respond to them.

The researchers found the following ten factors representing the basic motivations for attending ABE in Iowa. The terms themselves are derived from the research.

1. Self-improvement

2. Family Responsibilities

3. Diversion

4. Literacy Development

5. Community/Church Involvement

6. Job Advancement

7. Launching

8. Economic Need

9. Educational Advancement

10. Urging of Others

ABE students participate because they wish to improve themselves. Self-improvement includes such things as wanting to learn new things, being more independent, and wanting to be more intelligent. They are also motivated by a desire to meet Family Responsibilities, by serving as better examples to their children, and by being better parents. Diversion, a desire to dispel boredom, to meet new people, and to try something new, was found to motivate participation as does Literacy Development, a desire to read, write, and communicate better.

ABE students wish to be more successful in Community/ Church Involvement by helping more in church, and by being smarter voters and shoppers. They are motivated to achieve Job Advancement and to effectively negotiate life transitions into full adulthood by Launching themselves. Some ABE students are motivated by Economic Need which includes earning more money, entering job training, and getting off welfare. Educational Advancement motivates those who desire to further their educations and some participate simply because of the Urging of Others.

The "importance" of each factor was assessed by computing the mean item mean, the average of all item scores for the factor. Educational Advancement was found to be the most important motivation with a mean item mean of 2.55. Self-improvement was a close second with a mean item mean of 2.49, and Literacy Development was third.

The motivational profile of Iowa ABE students conflicts with some elements of general theory and descriptive research and supports others. In regard to conflicting elements, it is important to note that there is no evidence of a needs hierarchy at work. Quite to the contrary, components of Self-improvement such as wanting to learn new things (mean = 2.86), improving one's self (mean = 2.60), and becoming more intelligent (mean = 2.71) are higher order motivations in Maslow's terms and are ranked more highly than getting off welfare (mean = 1.65) or finding work (mean = 2.0) which might be considered lower order survival needs. Were there a hierarchy of needs/motivations operating, the situation would be reversed.

Miller's model and the deficiency orientation of the congruence model suggest that low literate adults may be socially alienated and therefore reluctant to participate in adult literacy education, or in any adult education for that matter. This is not borne out by the Iowa research which finds that a desire to participate more effectively in the community, church, and family is important motivation for participating in adult literacy education. These desires are hardly indicative of social alienation.

The Iowa data supports Johnstone and Rivera's finding that "to become a better person" is the most important motivator for taking courses; this suggests that ABE students do not differ greatly from the general population in respect to the motivating power of self-improvement. Yet the ABE population seems to differ from Johnstone and Rivera's population in respect to the importance of vocational motivators; vocational concerns are of less significance for ABE students.

The ten motivations for attending ABE in Iowa fit nicely with Carp, Peterson, and Roelf's five most important motivators. As the reader may recall, the authors' two most highly ranked motivators for would-be learners were to become better informed and to become a happier person. These can be conceived as being part of the global ABE motivator, Self-improvement. Carp, Peterson, and Roelf's third, fourth, and fifth most important motivators are as follows: to satisfy curiosity; to be a better parent/spouse; and to become a better citizen. The parallels to the ABE motivators Diversion, Family Responsibility, and Community/Church Involvement are clear and obvious.

What is most interesting, perhaps, is the basic correspondence between the motivational orientation literature which applies to adults in general and the motivations of ABE students. It must be remembered that the motivational orientation literature associated with Boshier and his replicators grounds its items in the theory of Cyril Houle while the Iowa ABE study grounded its items in a qualitative analysis of open ended interviews with ABE students. Hence, given the differences in approaches and populations, major differences might be expected. This does not seem to be the case. Boshier found five motivational orientations:

1. Escape Stimulation
2. Professional Advancement
3. Social Welfare
4. External Expectations
5. Cognitive Interest

In the Iowa ABE study, Boshier's Escape-Stimulation finds its parallel in Diversion. Professional Advancement links with Job Advancement; Social Welfare is quite compatible with the ABE motivators Family Responsibilities and Community/Church Involvement; External Expectations is closely paralleled by the Urging of Others, and major components of Boshier's Cognitive Interest motivator are found in the ABE motivation, Self-improvement.

The Iowa data on motivation to participate in ABE leads to two basic conclusions. First, ABE students are motivated by a wide range of factors which go far beyond literacy development or vocational mobility, although these are important. Motivations include the desire to become better people and more effective citizens. Some ABE students participate simply for the sake of diversion; others enroll because they are urged to. Still others wish to further their educations or satisfy economic needs. Second, and in our view more importantly, a comparison between ABE motivations and those of the general population—as derived from large scale and frequently replicated studies—indicates that there are very few differences between the two groups. In terms of the content of motivation, ABE students are like any other students who volunteer for learning. Given this, it is difficult to fathom how ABE students can be typified as being motivationally deficient.

Other Research

While there has been a considerable amount of discussion about what low literate adults need to learn, aside from the Iowa studies there has been very little research which focuses directly on ABE students' motivations for learning. Two large scale qualitative studies are notable, those of Mezirow, Darkenwald, and Knox (1975) and of Fingeret (1985).

Mezirow, Darkenwald, and Knox note six motivational types among ABE students:

1. Job Careerists

2. Concerned Mothers

3. Self-improvers

4. Educational Careerist

5. Troubled Youth

6. Educated Aliens

Job Careerists are motivated by a desire to upgrade their jobs, and they perceive the GED as the means of doing so. Concerned Mothers participate so that they can become better role models to their children and help their children with homework. Self-improvers are motivated by self-improvement. The Educational Careerist "places a high value on education. And, like the job careerist, he is interested in a good job—in the future" (p. 45). For the present, educational careerists focus on achieving a GED and perhaps furthering their educations. Troubled Youth is the fifth motivational type, and these learners participate simply because they have nothing else to do or because they are induced to attend. Members of the final group, Educated Aliens, are motivated by a desire to communicate better.

From her data, Fingeret (1985) concludes that reasons or personal goals are not fundamental for participation. What is fundamental is application contexts. "In other words, these [application contexts] are tasks, roles or functions requiring reading and writing skills that are confronting adults at this point in their lives. They hope that ABE program participation will enable, but not be limited to, accomplishment of these applications" (p. 59).

Fingeret links application contexts to the learner's life cycle status, thereby raising the possibility that motivation to participate in adult literacy may be associated with the learner's age set status. Motivations for teenagers derive from the struggle to make the tran-

sition into full adulthood. In the twenties, ABE students are motivated by the competing demands of work, family, and community.
ABE students in their thirties are motivated by a desire to be better
role models for others and for general self-fulfillment. In their mid-
forties and fifties, ABE students are increasingly motivated by "realizing old dreams," and in their sixties motivation is "often the
intrinsic reward of continuing to learn; after all these years, they
would like the self-satisfaction of learning to read or obtaining a
high school diploma" (p. 72).

The effect of age set on motivation to participate in ABE is
supported by Bova's (1985) research. Following the motivational
orientation tradition established by Boshier, Bova administered the
Educational Participation Scale (EPS) to 157 New Mexico ABE and
ESL students. She investigated four motivational factors.

1. Escape Stimulation

2. Professional Advancement

3. External Expectations

4. Personal Growth

Motivations were found to be associated with age. Emphasis on
Escape Stimulation, for example, was moderate during younger
ages, dropped from age 46–55 and increased during the years 55–
60. Similarly, concern about Professional Advancement was found
to be above average between 18 and 33, very high between 33 and
50 and lower in later years.

Summary

The research, although not extensive, presents a fairly clear
picture of what ABE students' motivations for participation are.
The Iowa research has identified ten motivations: Self-improvement, Family Responsibilities, Diversion, Literacy Development,
Community/Church Involvement, Job Advancement, Launching,
Economic Need, Educational Advancement, and the Urging of Others. It has been demonstrated that these ten motivations fit well
conceptually when collapsed into the more parsimonious motivational orientations derived from general research on the topic.
The ten motivations are also quite compatible with other,

rather sparse, research conducted on ABE students. Iowa's Job Advancement and Economic Need link with Mezirow, Darkenwald, and Knox's (1975) Job Careerist type; Family Responsibilities parallels the Concerned Mother; Self-improvement is synonymous with the Self-improver; Educational Advancement fits with the Educational Careerist.

The second conclusion is that, given the close correspondence between the findings of general motivational orientation research and the research specific to ABE, it can be inferred that in respect to kinds of motivation exhibited, ABE students differ very little from the general population.

Finally, it is important to note that motivational content seems to be influenced by the learner's position in the life cycle, with certain motivations being more or less important at different points.

CHAPTER 4

Nonparticipation

Federal data shows that in 1988 only 8% of those eligible for adult literacy education participated (Pugsley, 1990). This is true despite the fact that programs are free and the benefits of literacy are clear. Why? Obviously, answers are needed if we are to deal with the problem, and to a great extent these answers lie in an understanding of the nonparticipation phenomenon.

Clearly, if participation is to occur adults must be motivated to participate; desirable program offerings must be available and participation must not be constrained by conditions which make participation difficult or impossible. If any of these three conditions does not hold, the likelihood of participation is substantially reduced. In addition, the greater the motivation to participate, the more likely it is that adults will overcome constraining factors. As we will see, this logic permeates 35 years of research and theory on nonparticipation.

The approach of this chapter will be basically the same as that of the previous chapter. First what is known about nonparticipation in general will be reviewed. Then the discussion will move to a specific treatment of nonparticipation in adult literacy education.

GENERAL DESCRIPTIVE RESEARCH

Barriers to Participation

Much of the empirical research on nonparticipation is descriptive; it has focused on identifying factors which constrain participation, termed "barriers" or "deterrents," without attempting to generate or to connect with theory. The descriptive tradition begins with the first large scale study which probed barriers to participation, Johnstone and Rivera's *Volunteers for Learning* (1965).

Johnstone and Rivera

As part of their larger study which has been mentioned previously, Johnstone and Rivera asked their adult research subjects to respond to ten reasons for not attending adult education classes. These reasons varied from such things as "couldn't afford it," "too busy," and "too tired at night," to "don't know of available courses," "would feel childish," "feel too old to learn," and "don't need classes."

Nearly half (48%) of Johnstone and Rivera's respondents indicated that cost and lack of time were barriers, and, as we will see, this finding is borne out in subsequent research. Being too tired at night was mentioned by 45%; lack of information regarding classes was reported by 35%, and not needing classes was mentioned by only 12%.

Yet although Johnstone and Rivera's findings are important, it is their rudimentary classification scheme which has had the greatest lasting impact. They state, "Two main types of barriers to participation may be identified in the list of statements: influences more or less external to the individual or at least beyond the individual's control and those based on personal attitude or disposition toward participation" (p. 214). These two types were labeled situational and dispositional barriers. Cost is an example of a situational barrier; feeling childish represents a dispositional barrier.

Identifying barriers in itself, however, is a relatively meaningless activity unless we know to whom they apply. After all, society is far from homogeneous and barriers that function for some groups might not function for others. Recognizing this, Johnstone and Rivera went on to analyze the relationship between barriers to participation and sociodemographic factors, and they found significant associations. Women were more likely than men to be constrained by not being able to get out of their homes at night and by being too tired. Younger adults were more constrained by the cost of participation and older adults were limited by feeling too old. In respect to socioeconomic status, those of low socioeconomic status were much more constrained by not knowing of available classes; those of high socioeconomic status were more impeded by being too busy.

In general, older adults were more constrained by dispositional factors than younger adults, and younger adults were slightly more deterred by situational factors. Women were more constrained by situational barriers than men, and adults of low socioeconomic status were more constrained by both situational and dispositional factors than were adults of higher socioeconomic status.

The importance of Johnstone and Rivera's work to adult literacy education is that it provides a basic framework for analyzing the nonparticipation of low literate adults. Like all adults, the participation of low literate adults is constrained by a blend of attitudinal (dispositional) and situational factors. Yet, as Johnstone and Rivera demonstrate, socioeconomic status mediates the constraining factors to the extent that some barriers, such as lack of information, affect low literate adults more, and other barriers affect them less. Furthermore, within the low literate population such variables as age and gender play an important role in nonparticipation. Thus, as a population, low literate adults should not be treated as one homogeneous group. Quite to the contrary, the population is comprised of many subgroups which may be expected to react toward adult literacy education in different ways.

Carp, Peterson, and Roelfs

A major issue in descriptive research is the degree to which the results hold up over time. Thus replication of studies in different time periods is necessary if we are to make solid conclusions and to identify trends. In the tradition of Johnstone and Rivera, in 1972 Carp, Peterson, and Roelfs (Cross & Valley, 1974) conducted another large scale descriptive study of participation which generally confirmed previous research. This time the researchers' list of barriers to participation included 25 items. As with Johnstone and Rivera, the two most highly ranked barriers were cost, reported by 53% of the sample, and time constraints, reported by 46% of the sample. Interestingly, only 16% of those responding felt that lack of information about offerings was a deterrent.

Following with an analysis of the relationships between sociodemographics and barriers, Carp et al. found that twice as many men as women indicated job responsibilities as a barrier, while women were much more likely to mention home responsibilities. Men more often reported lack of time as a barrier, while women more often indicated that being too tired constrained participation.

Cost was a more substantial barrier for adults under 35, and reports of feeling too old and lack of energy increased with age.

Caucasians reported insufficient time and home responsibilities twice as often as blacks, while blacks were considerably more deterred by such things as low grades, not meeting requirements, cost, lack of child care, and lack of transportation.

Taken together, the work of Johnstone and Rivera and Carp et al. clearly demonstrates that barriers do not operate in isolation. Quite to the contrary, they derive from the press of life's responsibilities and the attitudes toward education which vary according to race, class, and gender. For less affluent groups such as blacks and the young, cost is a major barrier. For the full time employed, a chronic lack of time seems to be a critical factor.

Cross

Based on a review of the research on barriers to participation which drew heavily on Johnstone and Rivera and Carp et al., in 1981 Cross developed her own classification scheme. For Cross, barriers fall into three categories: situational barriers, institutional barriers, and dispositional barriers. As with Johnstone and Rivera, situational barriers pertain to constraints that are beyond the learner's control, and dispositional barriers relate to attitudes and feelings about adult education. Institutional barriers are a new category, however, and "consist of all those practices and procedures that exclude or discourage working adults from participating in educational activities" (p. 98). Adding institutional barriers to the classification was significant for, in doing so, Cross recognized that adult education institutions themselves contribute to the nonparticipation problem when they adopt policies, such as inconvenient scheduling and unrealistic course requirements, which make participation by adults difficult.

Cross concludes that situational barriers are the most severe and that cost and lack of time head the list. The magnitude of these barriers, however, may be influenced by the "alibi factor," a bias which may be inherent in the research methodologies employed in the studies. Most of the descriptive research is based on surveys or interviews in which respondents are asked why they have not participated. Yet education is considered by most to be a positive thing —indeed almost a responsibility—and many respondents may have responded with socially desirable reasons to explain why they failed to participate rather than expressing their real reasons.

Cross divides institutional barriers into five groups: scheduling problems, problems with location or transportation, lack of interesting or relevant courses, procedural problems, and lack of information about offerings. Regarding dispositional barriers, Cross notes that the research suggests these barriers are generally the less severe of the other three types but, as mentioned above, the "real" importance of dispositional barriers may be distorted by the alibi factor.

It may be that Cross's identification of institutional barriers is her greatest contribution to an understanding of nonparticipation in adult literacy education in that, among all barriers, institutional barriers are hypothetically the most amenable to the control of adult literacy programs. Clearly, scheduling, transportation, program appeal, and information about offerings are important. Indeed, most adult literacy professionals understand this (Mezirow, Darkenwald, & Knox, 1975). Yet, given the resources available for adult literacy education, substantial further reductions in institutional barriers may be beyond current capacity.

Darkenwald and Merriam

Efforts to categorize barriers did not end with Cross. Darkenwald and Merriam (1982) refine Cross's three part classification by proposing four types of barriers: situational, institutional, informational, and psychosocial. Situational and institutional barriers are essentially the same as Cross's counterparts. Informational barriers pertain to a lack of information about adult education offerings and, according to the authors, are most severe for disadvantaged adults.

Psychosocial barriers derive from the values and attitudes adults hold for adult education, and they are similar to dispositional barriers. In proposing a new term, however, the authors refine the dispositional barrier concept noting that psychosocial barriers are associated with socioeconomic status, that the components are multiple and complex, and that most can be placed in two categories.

The first category "encompasses negative evaluations of the usefulness, appropriateness, and pleasurability of engaging in adult education. Particularly among lower- and working-class persons, adult education may be seen as having little intrinsic value and little usefulness as a means of achieving personal goals" (p. 139).

The second category includes adults' negative evaluations of themselves as learners, and while it is noted that such barriers are less related to socioeconomic status than attitudes about adult education, "they are nonetheless prevalent among disadvantaged and working-class adults" (p. 139). Negative self-evaluation as learners includes such things as fear of failure and low self-efficacy.

The addition of the psychosocial dimension to the classification of barriers and its elaboration are important in that the category emphasizes the relationship between nonparticipation and class oriented value systems. What is not clear, however, is the precise object of the negative attitudes which adults of low socioeconomic status hold. Do negative evaluations about the usefulness of education and negative self-evaluations of themselves as learners pertain to learning in general, or do they pertain more narrowly to a formal school context? The answer is critical, for if learning itself is the object, this barrier is extremely difficult to deal with. Yet if, as Quigley (1989, 1990b) suggests, the object is *school*, it may be possible to understand the deep meanings which school represents for low socioeconomic status adults and to develop institutional contexts that are devoid of the negative aspects.

Deterrents Research

Up to the early 1980s the literature on barriers was primarily absorbed with describing what they were, assessing their magnitude, and classifying them intuitively. Indeed, it can be argued that none of the work between 1966 and 1980 added much to what Johnstone and Rivera found in 1965. After 1980, however, research on factors which inhibit participation took a new turn. First, the term "barrier" was replaced with the concept "deterrent." Although the terms are nearly synonymous, there are perhaps some subtle differences. Barriers were conceived to be factors which prevented otherwise motivated adults from participating—against their will, so to speak. The deterrent concept, however, subsumes motivational factors within it. Thus, in the deterrent tradition, one can be deterred by lack of motivation.

More importantly, the methodology changed in important ways. Rather than developing lists of barriers intuitively or replicating the lists of others, deterrents researchers tend to ground their research in the population studied by generating items qualitatively from open ended interviews. Then, instead of developing intuitive classification schemes, deterrents researchers tend to employ clustering procedures such as factor analysis which group deterrents according to their statistical properties.

Scanlan and Darkenwald (1984), for example, identified deterrents to participation among allied health care professionals. Data was collected using a 40-item Deterrents to Participation Scale (DPS) constructed from interview data gathered from 21 allied health professionals. The DPS was then administered to 750 allied health professionals of whom 479 responded for a response rate of 70%.

After subjecting the DPS items to factor analysis, the authors found six deterrents. The first was termed Disengagement to reflect component items which suggested inertia, boredom, uncertainty, etc. The second factor was labeled Lack of Quality, including such items as "because the program(s) tend to be of poor quality" and "because the program sponsors had a poor reputation." The third factor was termed Family Constraints because of the large number of items which related to conflicts revolving around respondents' family roles. Factor four was labeled Cost; the fifth factor was termed Lack of Benefit and included reasons for lack of participation such as "because there are no monetary benefits to be gained by attendance" and "because there are better things to spend my time and money on." The last factor, Work Constraints, was made up of items which reflected the conflicts of the workplace.

One issue which plagued earlier descriptive work was the lack of an analysis focusing on whether the barriers identified actually affected participation and, if so, to what degree. Scanlan and Darkenwald addressed this problem by regressing their deterrents on a measure of participation. They found that, taken together, the six deterrents accounted for nearly 40% of the variance. Clearly, at least for the study sample, deterrents have a substantial impact.

One problem with deterrents research is that it is not appropriate to generalize the results obtained with one population to another or to the adult population as a whole. This is so for two reasons. First, since questionnaire items are grounded in the population studied, different studies employ different instrumentation. Second, even when the same instruments are used on different populations, the results of factor analysis can vary greatly.

In order to deal with this limitation, Darkenwald and Valentine (1985) developed a version of the Deterrents to Participation

Scale (DPS-G) for the general population, following essentially the same procedures for survey construction employed by Scanlan and Darkenwald. The DPS-G was mailed to a random sample of 2,000 New Jersey households, and 215 responses were obtained for a response rate of 10.7%. After factor analysis, the authors again found six factors:

1. Lack of Confidence

2. Lack of Course Relevance

3. Time Constraints

4. Low Personal Priority

5. Cost

6. Personal Problems

At the .001 level, Lack of Confidence was found to correlate with age and educational attainment. Cost was associated with gender, age, educational attainment and income, and Personal Problems was associated with gender. The other factors lacked substantial relationships with sociodemographic variables.

In 1988 Darkenwald replicated the general population research on a British sample (Darkenwald, 1988). The author concludes, "Despite significant modifications made to the version of the DPS-G used in Britain, the factor analytic findings were remarkably similar for the two countries. In brief, the British analysis yielded an additional factor (seven vs. six) and 'broke down' the U.S. factor labeled 'Lack of Confidence' into two more refined factor structures" (p. 129).

Deterrents to participation were also studied by Martindale and Drake (1989) and by Blais, Duquette, and Painchaud (1989). Martindale and Drake, in a study of air force personnel, found the following basic deterrents to participation in off duty adult education:

1. Lack of Course Relevance

2. Lack of Confidence

3. Cost and Time Constraints

4. Lack of Convenience

5. Lack of Interest

6. Family Problems

7. Lack of Encouragement

In a sample of diplomaed nurses Blais et al. found five factors:

1. Incidental Costs

2. Low Priority for Work Related Activities

3. Absence of External Incentives

4. Irrelevance of Additional Formal Education for Professional Practice

5. Lack of Information and Affective Support

After nearly thirty-five years of research on factors which constrain participation in adult education, what do we know? Scanlan (1986) offers an answer. After an extensive review of the deterrent literature, Scanlan concludes it is now clear that "Deterrents to participation is a multidimensional concept, subsuming several logical groupings of psychological, social, and environmental variables. Also clear is the realization that these variables are associated with the perceptions of prospective learners. Additionally, it is evident that the perceived magnitude of these variables *is* associated with adults' participation behavior. Lastly, and of most practical importance, is the knowledge that the impact of these variables on participation behavior varies according to both personal characteristics and life circumstances of the individual" (p. 35).

Scanlan goes on to present a synthesis of the factors which have been found to deter participation, concluding that the research suggests eight basic deterrents:

1. Individual, family, or home related problems (e.g., child care, poor health, transportation difficulties)

2. Cost concerns, including opportunity costs and lack of financial assistance

3. Questionable worth, relevance, or quality of available educational opportunities

4. Negative perceptions regarding the value of education in general, including those related to prior unfavorable experience

5. Lack of motivation or indifference toward learning (e.g., anomie, apathy)

6. Lack of self-confidence in one's learning abilities, including lack of social support/encouragement

7. A general proclivity towards nonaffiliation (e.g., marginal involvement in social activities)

8. Incompatibilities of time and/or place, especially those associated with conflicting demands of work (p. 35)

Despite the fact that deterrents research certainly informs the nonparticipation issue, there are limitations to this line of inquiry which merit mention. The first is that virtually all the deterrents research has been based on learners' expressed perceptions of the factors which deter them. It may well be, however, that potential learners are deterred by factors they are not aware of, factors which, because they are not "perceived," have not been identified as being critical to nonparticipation. It may also be that in recounting their perceptions of deterrents, research subjects tend to reply with socially acceptable answers. To the extent that this is true, assessments of the magnitude of particular deterrents such as cost must be taken with some skepticism.

The second limitation to deterrents research is that it is essentially atheoretical and perhaps even conceptually confused. It is atheoretical because it is based in descriptive research—research which, because of the methodologies employed, may not be generalized from one population to another nor connected to a larger body of theory. Because of this problem, the predictive power of deterrents research is somewhat diminished. It may be conceptually confused in that the relationship between deterrents and motivation is not clear. Are deterrents factors which impede participation by adults who are motivated to learn? Or is lack of motivation a deterrent in its own right? It is important to resolve the issue if deterrents research is to reach its full potential by linking with theories of motivation such as expectancy-valence or Cross's Chain of Response.

It is also clear from the research on deterrents that the factors which constrain participation are considerably influenced by sociodemographic factors. Both Johnstone and Rivera and Carp, Peterson, and Roelfs, for example, find a relationship between young age and cost while Johnstone and Rivera note that low-SES adults are considerably more deterred by lack of information regarding offerings, and high-SES adults are more likely to be impeded by time constraints. Given the considerable impact of sociodemographic variables on deterrents, it may be that a basic understanding of deterrents to participation provides only general guidance in understanding why low literate adults in specific fail to participate in adult literacy education.

RESEARCH AND THEORY
APPLIED TO LOW LITERATE ADULTS

Although, as we will see, there is a scarcity of empirical research which focuses directly on the nonparticipation of low literate adults, there are at least two theoretical orientations which are useful in pinpointing problems and exploring solutions: marketing theory and resistance theory. Before we address theory and research on the nonparticipation of low literate adults, however, it is important to frame the problem.

Hunter and Harman (1979) summarize the basic problem of nonparticipation in adult literacy very nicely. They state, "Educators often speak of 'target populations,' meaning all those who might legitimately be considered candidates for certain programs. During the last decade the approximately 60 million American adults who had not completed high school were designated the target population for ABE and a host of smaller programs designed to promote literacy or provide credentials. The term *demand population* refers to those who actually enroll in these programs, a group estimated at between 2 and 4 million adults in the United States. The 50 million-plus gap between the target and demand population is perceived as a major challenge to adult educators. How can it be narrowed? How can a larger proportion of the approximately 60 million 'targets' be motivated to enroll in the program? Of course, these questions assume that everyone should be literate and that everyone without a high school diploma should seek one" (p. 58).

A failure to reach nonparticipants represents two basic costs. First it represents a social cost in that the total productivity of contemporary society depends on a literate population. We have all heard how our schools are failing, how we are producing illiterate adults faster than adult education programs can educate them. Clearly, the social cost of low literacy will not be reduced unless the proportion of literate adults to low literate adults is improved substantially. Second, to the extent that lack of literacy restricts individual social mobility—and federal adult education policy has always assumed that it does—low literacy represents a significant individual cost to low literates themselves.

Marketing Theory

Marketing theory represents a perspective which has value for analyzing the nonparticipation of low literate adults (Beder, 1986, 1980; Scanlan, 1986; Kerka, 1986). In such a perspective, nonparticipation is linked to demand, and the relationship between demand and nonparticipation has already been drawn in the previous chapter. To recapitulate briefly, for demand to be positive—for adults to be willing to exchange their resources to partake in program offerings—potential learners must want the offering, must perceive that the provider can deliver the offering, and must prefer the offering over any of its competitors. Demand can actually be negative; potential learners may actively avoid participation. There can also be no demand, as when potential learners are indifferent, and positive demand, when participation is likely in the absence of substantial deterrents. Given this line of reasoning, the key to dealing with nonparticipation is to increase the level of demand for adult literacy education.

There are at least five "variables" which need to be taken into account if demand is to be enhanced: competition, program offerings, price, promotion, and location. We will begin with competition.

Competition

Generally speaking, adult educators think of other competing programs when they consider competition, but there appears to be no evidence that this kind of competition is a factor in nonpartici- pation. In fact, it would be so only if there were so many adult literacy programs that none could sustain adequate enrollments. Competition, however, has other forms. Kotler (1975) notes three.

The first is generic competition which "refers to other broad product categories that might satisfy the same need" (p. 59). At issue are other kinds of activities that might satisfy the same needs that literacy education does. There are several possibilities. Fingeret (1983) notes that low literate adults often satisfy their need to read by es- tablishing social networks which include individuals who read for them. Thus the friends and relatives who read for low literate adults are competing with literacy education in a very real sense.

Low literate adults sometimes develop compensating mecha- nisms which serve the function of reading and mathematics. In fact, the mechanisms which low literate adults establish to compensate for low literacy are lore in adult literacy circles. I am reminded of an illiterate painter whom I encountered during my dissertation re- search. Not being able to do basic arithmetic, he "computed" the area of a room by running a special stick along the appropriate sides of a wall and then "adding" the areas of the walls together. In es- sence he had invented mathematics for himself, and he claimed that his estimates were seldom inaccurate.

In analyzing the power of generic competition, the costs and benefits of becoming literate must be weighed against the costs and benefits of dealing with low literacy in other ways. For many, be- coming literate may be perceived as the most difficult and distasteful option for dealing with low literacy. Consequently, the business goes to the competition, so to speak.

There is sketchy evidence which suggests that by adopting strategies which compete with literacy education many adults are able to compensate effectively. For example, when the family in- comes of adults who participated in Iowa adult literacy programs were compared to those of nonparticipants (Beder, 1989a), it was found that on the average nonparticipants earned $23,502 and par- ticipants earned $11,194. While this data may be influenced by the fact that nonparticipants were considerably older on the average, they do suggest that, in respect to income, strategies which compete with literacy education may work rather well.

The second type of competition is product form competition and it refers to other versions of literacy education which may serve the same need. Thus, tutoring based models, learning centers, and classroom oriented instruction may at times compete with each other for students, but the net effect on nonparticipation is probably minimal.

The third type of competition is enterprise competition, and it refers to specific organizations or systems which compete with each other. To a certain extent the economic system itself may be in competition with adult literacy education. For example, for non-participants whose basic goal is job acquisition, there are two alternatives: acquire a job by first becoming literate, or acquire a job but without engaging in literacy education. When the economy is strong and jobs are available, literacy may not be essential in acquiring a job and earning a liveable income. Data from Iowa supports this (Beder, 1989a). When Iowa adults who were eligible for the state literacy program but had never attended were asked if their lives would have been any different if they had completed high school, about one third responded with "no." When asked why, 25% said they were pleased with their lives as they were, 20% noted that they were pleased with their jobs; 25% answered that they would be doing what they are now anyway, and 28% indicated that they did not need high school and it was not important to them. Thus it may well be that for many low literates the political economy provides well despite low literacy. It may also be, however, that many of the nonparticipants studied (defined in the study as those without high school) could actually read rather well.

The point here is, of course, that adult literacy education is not without competition. Quite to the contrary, there are other alternatives to becoming literate that may function well for many people. For those who are able to compensate for their low literacy, the demand for literacy education is likely to be quite low.

The Product

The second marketing factor which may affect nonparticipation pertains to the product itself, adult literacy program offerings. The adult literacy "product" has two dimensions: the tangible product—the part that learners can touch and see—and the core product (Beder, 1980). The core product represents the basic benefit that learners seek from participating. Let us first examine the tangible product.

As was noted in the first chapter, for many reasons the federal adult literacy program is strongly associated with the public schools. Nationally, the majority of classes are conducted in schools; teachers tend to have had public school experience, and the technology of instruction is school based. Thus most of the things that adult literacy education students can see and touch are associated with schools.

For many potential adult literacy education participants, however, public school was an unpleasant experience and dropping out was fraught with anguish. For example, nearly one third of the Iowa nonparticipants studied indicated that either failing to complete courses/getting behind, parental interference, pregnancy, personal conflicts with school, or dislike for school was the major reason for dropping out (Beder, 1989a). For them "school" may represent past failure and personal turmoil to the extent that the "schoolness" of adult literacy education seriously diminishes the demand for it.

It is possible that the core product of adult literacy education also influences demand. As explained earlier, the core product pertains to the basic benefit consumers seek in purchasing a product or service. When purchasing a luxury automobile, for example, the core product is status and prestige, and in purchasing diet drinks the core product may be a slender body rather than pleasant taste. Generally speaking, the core product has as much, or greater, influence on the demand for a product than does the tangible product.

What is the core product for adult literacy education? The Iowa Participant Study (Beder & Valentine, 1987) found that there are ten basic benefits (or motivations) that adult literacy education students seek from attending: Self-Improvement, the ability to better meet Family Responsibilities, Diversion, Literacy Development, more effective Community/Church Involvement, Job Advancement, Launching into mainstream society, meeting Economic Needs, Educational Advancement, and satisfying the Urging of Others. The desired benefits are many and they go well beyond the mere acquisition of a diploma.

But do potential participants perceive that adult literacy education can and will provide these benefits? Herein lies the issue in respect to the core product. It may well be that adult literacy programs present themselves too narrowly to potential learners—as programs which have reading and writing as their only benefits. It may also be that many nonparticipants do not perceive literacy as being the best avenue to acquiring desired benefits. Being a conscientious worker may be perceived as being a more effective strategy for job advancement, for example, and many may fail to see a connection between literacy and the meeting of family responsibilities.

Price

Price may also affect nonparticipation. Price includes two dimensions: the actual dollar cost and the opportunity costs, defined as the value of those things one must forgo to participate, such as time away from work or family. In respect to dollar cost, most adult literacy programs do not charge fees. Yet the impact of "free" instruction on nonparticipation is open to question. Research on the issue is sparse and inconclusive. Olds (1952) found that the absence of a fee enhanced participation among low income adults in public school adult education programs, but in a study of community adult school participants, Boshier (1979) concluded that while lack of a fee generally enhanced participation, "participants in fee courses manifested similar characteristics to those of non-fee participants" (p. 161). Unwillingness to pay a fee, then, did not distinguish socially disadvantaged groups from others.

It is quite likely, however, that the major costs of participation pertain to opportunity costs such as a diversion of effort from solving family problems, getting a job (Hayes, 1988), or dealing with the demands of work (Beder, 1989a). Adult literacy students, unlike their preadult counterparts, must perform a multiplicity of roles. Accordingly, by necessity they must divide their efforts between their families, communities, and work. When the demands of these other arenas of effort are high, the opportunity costs of participation increase and may result in nonparticipation.

Promotion

Promotion, or the lack of it, may be another factor in nonparticipation. Promotion, which is persuasive communication directed at stimulating participation, has typically taken three forms in adult literacy education: advertising which is planned and paid for by the adult literacy provider, publicity which is orchestrated news coverage, and direct sales such as the use of door to door recruiters. Early efforts at television advertising were piloted by Project Reach in 1972 (McClelland, 1972), and most adult literacy professionals are familiar with the large scale advertising and publicity effort orchestrated by the PLUS project during recent years.

Door to door recruiters have been employed in many states (Mezirow, Knox, & Darkenwald, 1975; Beder, 1974) with varying degrees of success.

Nevertheless, there is little evidence that promotion has had a great impact on nonparticipation. There are three possible reasons. First it may be that promotional efforts have lacked quality. Falk (1986), for example, notes that for promotion to be effective it must entail a mix of methods carefully blended into a coherent total strategy. Yet most promotional efforts in adult literacy education seem to have been sporadic and haphazard. Second, it may be that insufficient resources have been allocated to promotion. In commenting on promotional budgets, Falk (1986) states, "First, organizations should spend no more or no less than the amount necessary to attract and enroll the desired number of students in the activity being promoted" (p. 53). Given the chronically low level of funding for the federal adult literacy program, however, most resources have been allocated to the direct delivery of service rather than to promotional efforts. Finally, it may be that for many of the reasons we have discussed there is very little demand for adult literacy education among those who are eligible. Lacking the will to participate, nonparticipants may simply resist promotional efforts.

Location

Two attributes of program location may bear on nonparticipation: accessibility and the symbolic value of the location. Regarding accessibility, the importance of an accessible location to participation in adult education has been noted many times from Johnstone and Rivera (1965) to Mason (1986). Inner city blacks, for example, often lack automobiles and must spend scarce resources on taxis unless literacy programs are located on a public transportation route (Stack, 1974). Rural adults may have to drive many miles to classes after a long day's work. Mezirow, Darkenwald, and Knox (1975) suggest outreach centers as a means of ameliorating the problem of accessibility, but outreach is frequently limited by a need to have a minimum number of students available for instruction and by a lack of funding. Distance education through television has also been tried but with limited success (Larson, 1980). It may well be, then, that many nonparticipants fail to attend simply because lack of accessibility restricts the opportunity.

It may be that a dramatic increase of resources for adult literacy will be needed if we are to make substantial progress on the accessibility problem. This may be less so, however, for the symbolic aspects of location. The locations where adult literacy education is conducted convey an image and, to a certain extent, the values and attitudes which low literates ascribe to literacy programs pertain to the location. After all, the location may be the most visible aspect of the program for nonparticipants who have never entered an adult literacy classroom. What is the symbolic "message" of adult literacy locations? Irish (1980) notes that "The least educated adults may, in many instances, have experienced chronic failure in school. For this reason, they may be fearful of returning to that setting." Schools may also convey childishness and harsh authority. In respect to authority, Beder (1979) notes that while the Adult Education Act itself imposes few restrictions on local programs, restrictions are added at the state and local level to the extent that the same regulations which apply to children are often imposed on adult literacy students—no smoking, no alcohol, no food in the classroom, and the day teacher's bulletin board and seating arrangement are inviolate. Other settings may also convey symbolic messages. Members of other faiths may react negatively to specific church locations, and the workplace for some may symbolize toil and constraints on freedom. Nonparticipation, then, may be abetted by the negative symbolism which is attached to many adult literacy locations.

The Mix

Just as a marketing orientation is useful for analyzing and understanding nonparticipation, it can suggest strategies for dealing with the problem. The practical objective in a marketing approach is to "mix" the kinds of variables discussed here into a well articulated strategy. Promotion alone, for example, is unlikely to be successful unless at the same time programs are made more attractive, locations are accessible and appealing, and opportunity costs are reduced. Furthermore, as Willard and Warren note (1986), strategies must apply and be coordinated at every level, from the state office to the classroom. A piecemeal ad hoc approach is not likely to have a substantial impact.

Resistance Theory

Resistance theory locates the roots of nonparticipation in the public school culture from which nonparticipants dropped out. It is a relatively new line of investigation, at least in respect to adult education, but in recognizing the connections between history, culture, and a reluctance to participate in adult literacy, it raises provocative issues. The basic argument is that for many youths there is a discontinuity between their culture of orientation and the culture of the school which is a reflection of the dominant, mainstream culture. The discontinuity in values, attitudes, and acceptable behaviors leads to conflict which the schools repress with exercises of authority. This leads to acts of resistance, and, in the ultimate act, the student drops out. Resistance to school and the culture it represents becomes deeply ingrained and the net result is a strong aversion to further schooling.

Quigley (1990b) analyzes resistance to schooling through "the eyes" of protagonists of ten American and Canadian novels. He concludes that it is not learning which is resisted by these literary characters but the infringement of rights and the perception of pointless injustice on the part of school officials. Additionally, Quigley finds that for these protagonists resistance takes place with varying degrees of visibility, that resisters are capable learners who want to learn, and that the process of resistance includes stages and sequenced steps of awareness.

Some fictional resisters seem to understand that their cultural values are at odds with the school and they are among the first to quit; others stay, rebel, lose their battle, and then drop out. Resistance increases as students become aware of the injustices imposed upon them and as they observe, compare, and begin to challenge the system. Finally they break away and, in doing so, experience "a euphoric sense of control over self and influence over others" (p. 113). Some eventually reconcile themselves "to the ones they left behind"; others never do.

Quigley's work is important in that it breaks ground and makes the link between nonparticipation and previous experience with public school, but it is also limited by its data source, the novel. In 1989, however, Quigley conducted an empirical study of twenty resisters which for the most part confirms his earlier work. A resister was defined as "one who is aware that a geographically, financially, and time-convenient ABE program is available and accessible but who consciously refuses to attend" (p. 2). After analyzing the twenty in depth interviews, Quigley identified three types of resisters: those who had experienced the school system as being insensitive, unsupportive, and abusive in its authority, those who found school to be irrelevant or insulting because their culture had been ignored or demeaned, and older adults who felt it was simply too late to return to school. Despite the fact that Quigley's subjects all resisted further schooling, most reported that they had enjoyed learning in school and that they highly valued education.

While Quigley tends to focus on resistance as an individual phenomenon, Paul Willis (1978) defines resistance as a cultural phenomenon in his ethnography of the Hammertown (England) lads. The lads are a group of close working class friends who represent the school counter culture. They oppose school authority and "invade" its values of diligence, deference, and respect in an effort to win symbolic and physical autonomy from the system. They also oppose and occasionally terrorize conformist students. The lads belittle and ridicule the system at every chance with practical jokes and the flagrant flaunting of authority. They exhibit a machismo sexism and racism, and they occasionally fight and steal. The system reacts with the elements of authority at its disposal, but at best it can only contain the lads and is itself changed.

The lads oppose the school with what amounts to internecine guerilla warfare, but why and to what end? In proposing answers Willis advances resistance theory. For Willis there are two contravening processes that are taking place at the same time in the Hammertown school, differentiation and integration. "*Differentiation* is the process whereby typical exchanges expected in the formal institutional paradigm are reinterpreted, separated, and discriminated with respect to working class interests, feelings, and meanings" (p. 62). "*Integration* is the opposite of *differentiation* and is the process whereby class oppositions and intentions are redefined, truncated, and deposited within sets of apparently legitimate institutional relationships and exchanges" (p. 63).

For Willis, the "typical exchanges" are guided by a value system. The school gives knowledge and qualifications and in return expects deference and obedience. But because of the working class values they hold, the lads value "doing" over mental activity. What really counts is how things work. To them qualifications are meaningless as all jobs are the same—labor for a pay envelope—and they believe that they know more about "laboring" than the school officials. The exchange breaks down, and so does the moral authority of the school for the lads. Consequently, in order to contain the lads, the school must resort to its axis (framework) of formal authority, its control over discipline, time schedules, and physical space, and the net result for the lads is that the school becomes a prison. The rebellion is fed.

It is through the processes which Willis describes that working class labor and subculture are reproduced. The lads all take manual jobs and fill the niche in the division of labor which others would seek to avoid. But for Willis, this is not an act devoid of choice and creativity. The lads choose their fate in belief that it is the correct path and are quite conscious of the choice. They come to their place in the social order through struggle which is at times quite creative. Yet, nevertheless, their destiny is a social destiny. As Willis states, "In another society 'the lads' would have been shown the way, they would not have discovered their own" (p. 121).

Giroux (1983) argues that a theory of resistance needs to recognize that domination is not static or complete. Rather, through human agency it is resisted and through resistance there is the potential for emancipation. It is important to understand how domination is resisted and what the implications of resistance are. How is resistance produced and how are its manifestations mediated by the ideological, linguistic, and material aspects of culture? How is the power which creates the resistance applied and to what social purposes?

Giroux might characterize the behavior of the lads as being merely oppositional, a "standing against" which precludes the potential for positive social transformation. Indeed, the lads' rebellion is fraught with racism, sexism, and self-destruction. The social order remains the same, and the lads take their place at the bottom of it. But how and why? Giroux argues the critical analysis of the sociocultural forces which foster the opposition may "unlock the act," thus creating the possibility for collective social action directed toward change. Oppositional struggle, thus informed, becomes resistance that leads to social transformation.

Emerging resistance theory leads to several propositions which bear upon nonparticipation in adult literacy education. First, nonparticipation for some may be a rational act which derives from an opposition to the *school culture* (not necessarily learning) which they resisted and then left at the point of dropout. Second, nonparticipation may be rooted in prior school experience. Hence an understanding of nonparticipation must take its sociohistorical context into account. Third, the production of school leavers who elect not

88   ADULT LITERACY

to return to schooling may be part of the social reproduction process. To the extent that this is true, nonparticipation fulfills a function in that it insures a supply of labor at the bottom tier. Because
of their lack of skills and cultural orientations, those who end up
there are likely to remain there. Finally, for those nonparticipants
who are resisters, school based approaches to adult literacy are not
likely to work, and, if we are to reach them, new approaches to
adult literacy education must be found.

There is some empirical evidence which supports a resistance
theory of nonparticipation. In a recent National Assessment of Educational Progress (NAEP) study of 3,600 adults between the ages of
21 and 25 (Kirsch & Junglebut, 1986, p. 47), school dropouts were
asked why they had not completed. Reasons included finances (2.5%),
work (18.4%), pregnancy (11.2%), boredom (36.5%), grades
(3.3%) and personal (27.1%). While finances, work, pregnancy,
and grades may or may not be related to resistance, boredom and
personal reasons strongly reflect the characteristics of resistance
noted by Quigley and Willis. Together these two reasons account
for over two thirds of the response.

                          Empirical Research

The empirical research literature which pertains directly to
nonparticipation in adult literacy education is sparse, probably because it is extremely difficult to obtain a representative sample of
low literate nonparticipants to study. Two studies merit mention:
Hayes's (1987,1988) study of deterrents to participation and the
nonparticipant portion of the Iowa Adult Literacy Studies (Beder,
1989a, 1990a).

The logic of Hayes's work is in the tradition of deterrents research discussed earlier. Work commenced with open ended interviews with teachers, teachers' aides, and adult literacy education
students who were asked to identify deterrents to participation. The
reasons thus collected were then formatted into a 32-item, Likert
formatted scale, which was administered to 160 students from seven
urban programs who were selected by their teachers as being representative of the adult literacy population. The deterrents to participation were then subjected to factor analysis to ascertain if an
underlying structure to nonparticipation could be identified.

Hayes found five factors. The first was Low Self-Confidence, and the six items which comprised it referred to the perceived difficulty of becoming more literate and to the feelings of inadequacy toward learning. The second factor, Social Disapproval, was so labeled after items such as "I felt that my friends or the people I work with wouldn't like it if I returned to school," "I felt that my family wouldn't like it if I returned to school," and "I didn't think I needed to read better."

Situational Barriers, the third factor, pertained to such things as the lack of child care and transportation and to family problems. Negative Attitudes Towards Classes related to learners' negative feelings toward adult literacy education, and the last factor, Low Personal Priority, was named after such items as "It was more important to get a job than go to school," and "I didn't have time to go to school."

Hayes's work demonstrates that adult literacy students are deterred by a wide array of factors which range from psychological traits (low self-confidence) and negative attitudes, to external constraints (situational barriers). Two conceptual flaws, however, limit confidence in the results. First, for logistical reasons, Hayes was unable to acquire a representative sample and thus the external validity of the research may have been compromised. Second, and more important, all of Hayes's subjects were enrolled in adult literacy education; they were not nonparticipants. Thus the subjects of the study on deterrents to participation was conducted on a sample who, by enrolling in adult literacy education, had demonstrated that they were not deterred.

The Iowa Nonparticipation Study (Beder, 1989a, 1990a) rectified some of Hayes's limitations, although the study was similar in the logic of its design. As with Hayes, items pertaining to nonparticipation were generated through qualitative interviews with 21 high school dropouts who had not attended adult literacy education. Likewise, the 32 items generated were subjected to factor analysis to identify an underlying structure to nonparticipation. The sampling procedure and survey administration were quite different, however.

In an effort to acquire a representative sample of Iowa citizens who were eligible for adult literacy education but had *never participated*, a screener survey was sent to a random sample of 9,000 adults. The survey asked several basic attitudinal questions regarding public education in general and then quite unobtrusively sought basic data pertaining to high school completion and age. Those who self-identified themselves as no longer attending public school, not having a high school diploma or GED, and never having attended ABE were asked to volunteer for a telephone interview with a promise of a five dollar payment for their time. Surveys were returned by 1321 individuals; 175 volunteers were obtained, and 129 telephone interviews with eligible nonparticipants were completed for a response rate of 74%.

The first objective of the Nonparticipation Study was to identify the reasons for nonparticipation in adult literacy education, and to this end the 32 nonparticipation items were subjected to factor analysis. Four basic reasons for nonparticipation resulted. Items such as "A high school diploma would not improve my life," and "I don't think I could use the things I would learn in school," defined the first factor as Low Perception of Need. The second factor, Perceived Effort, was so named after items which related to the mental ("School is too hard") and physical ("It would take me too long to finish") effort which respondents associated with participation. Dislike for School and Situational Barriers were the final two factors identified. An examination of the mean item scores for each factor indicates that Low Perception of Need (1.7), Perceived Effort (1.6), and Situational Barriers (1.7) are about equal in importance while Dislike for School is less important (1.4).

The second question posed by the study had to do with the relationships between reasons for nonparticipation and sociodemographic and background variables. When the factor scores for the four reasons for nonparticipation were correlated with sociodemographic and background variables, there were several statistically significant results (.01 level). Low Perception of Need was found to be associated with age ($r = .61$) and with other variables generally associated with age such as retirement ($r = .54$) and widowhood ($r = .35$). It may well be that as adults age they adapt to their state of low literacy, and perceived need for literacy education declines correspondingly.

Situational Variables correlated with marriage ($r = .24$) and full-time employment ($r = .23$), suggesting that the press of family and job are particularly important to this factor. Perceived Difficulty and Dislike for School, however, correlated with nothing at the .01 level, indicating that these reasons for nonparticipation crosscut sociodemographic groups.

In understanding nonparticipation, the relationship between age and Low Perception of Need may be especially important, and this is true for two reasons. First, it is very difficult to do anything about Low Perception of Need for, in terms of earlier analysis, this reason represents a state of no demand. Second, the bulk of the nonparticipant population is made up of older adults. While the mean age for Iowa participants was found to be 30, the mean age for nonparticipants was 57, and 42% were over age 65. Thus if nonparticipants are defined by those who lack high school, as was the case in the Iowa study, the great majority are likely to be older adults who are reluctant to enroll in adult literacy education simply because they feel they do not need it.

Although the study populations, sampling procedures, and terminology applied to the factors differ considerably between the Hayes and Iowa studies, there is a basic correspondence in findings. For example, many of the items which led Hayes to define her first factor as Low Self-Confidence—items relating to the difficulty of classes and not feeling smart enough—find parallels in the Iowa factor, Perceived Effort. It may be that self-confidence and perceived effort are linked, and it is the belief that adult literacy education will be arduous which breeds low self-confidence.

Both studies found that situational barriers are a factor in nonparticipation and, as our earlier discussion demonstrated, this holds true for many other populations of adults as well. Hayes's Negative Attitudes Towards Classes is quite similar to the Iowa Dislike For School factor, both conceptually and in the items which constitute the two factors. Finally, Hayes's Social Disapproval factor contains several items which relate to Low Perception of Need in the Iowa Study, items such as "I felt returning to school wouldn't help me," "I thought book learning wasn't important," and "I didn't think I needed to read better."

Taken together the two studies suggest two major constellations of reasons for nonparticipation. One is structural; the other is attitudinal. The structural component is represented by the situational barriers factors, and it suggests that nonparticipants are blocked or deterred by lack of many of the resources required for participation such as time, information, transportation, and child care. Yet more importantly, perhaps, is the fact that many of the most powerful reasons for nonparticipation stem from attitudes toward adult literacy education. Nonparticipants often feel that they don't need it or that it is too hard for them, and some simply do not like school.

CONCLUSION

Although the findings of the Iowa Nonparticipation Study are useful in their own right, Low Perception of Need, Perceived Difficulty, Situational Barriers, and Dislike for School can serve the double purpose of providing a framework for a summary analysis of nonparticipation in adult literacy education.

Low Perception of Need

Although it is clear than many low literate adults fail to participate in adult literacy education simply because they do not perceive the need, to leave it at that is overly simplistic. Why do they fail to perceive a need? There are several logical alternatives. First it may be that low literacy is just one more of the deficits which disadvantaged adults learn to compensate for in meeting their life goals. Once they adapt to low literacy, in a very real sense they do not need it, for it no longer seriously affects life functioning in ways they consider problematic. Although the available evidence suggests such an interpretation (Fingeret, 1983; Beder, 1989a), more research will be needed for such an interpretation to be conclusive.

It may also be that many of those who are identified as low literates because they have not completed high school or because they score low on tests can actually read quite well. In a study of the black elderly, Heisel and Larson (1984) make this point quite effectively. They state, "By Census Bureau standards, about half the population studied here would be classified as functionally illiterate and a quarter would be considered totally illiterate. . . . By their own standards, however, seventy percent of this group are average or better readers, and only ten to fifteen percent have any difficulty meeting the functional reading requirements of their social milieu" (p. 69). To the extent that those who are identified as nonparticipants can read well, the problem has more to do with misclassification than it does with a need to become literate.

It is equally possible, however, that nonparticipants do need literacy education but do not perceive that they do. Important here is the distinction between a social need and an individual need. Social policy argues that low literate adults need to be educated because lack of literacy impedes economic productivity and results in expensive transfer payments to the poor. Thus, to the extent that the reduction of low literacy benefits us all, they *do* need it. Yet, just because there is a social need, it does not follow that the individual need is perceived. Thus when we claim that 60 million adults "need" adult literacy and disparage the fact that only two to four million actually enroll (Hunter & Harman, 1979), what we are really saying is that *we* need them to need adult literacy.

If low literate adults do not perceive a need for literacy and indeed have no need, then the resolution of the issue is quite simple. We delete this group from the target population and have done with it. Yet there is a problem. As the resistance theorists note, needs are socially constituted. Willis' lads come to believe that they do not need qualifications, or "mental" knowledge. Not perceiving the need, they do not fulfill it and they end up functioning at the bottom level of society. Thus the manner in which needs are constructed in society is a critical issue in social equality. Are nonparticipants' perceptions that they do not need literacy education a social construction? Have they been induced by the processes of social reproduction not to need something very vital. If this is the case, to dismiss them from the target population would be a grave injustice.

There is one, final, observation that should be made in respect to Low Perception of Need. This factor has been shown to be associated with age (Beder, 1989a, 1990a) to the extent that older adults are considerably less likely to perceive the need. There are several possible explanations. It may be that as adults age, they adapt to low literacy. It may also be that many older adults were very successful learners during their youth but did not obtain high school diplomas for lack of opportunity in a bygone era. Lacking formal instruction, they simply learned to read on their own. Whatever the case, the point is this: Policy decisions which lead to a focus on the demand population—those low literates who do perceive the need for adult literacy—are likely to ignore a large portion of the older population. Is this desirable?

Perceived Effort

It is interesting to note that none of the deterrents research on literate populations has found that perceived effort is a factor in nonparticipation, although low self-confidence, which is a very common factor, sometimes includes elements of perceived effort. Why do adult literacy students perceive the effort to be considerable, while adults in other settings do not? Perhaps they are right, that the effort involved in becoming literate is perceived as, and *is*, a critical aspect of the enterprise. Perhaps this factor has not surfaced in the deterrents literature cited earlier because the adult education to which these studies refer has been of relatively short duration.

Adult literacy education is protracted; the material is abstract, and there are often few benchmarks by which learners can chart their progress. These factors contribute to the actual effort required. Moreover, nonparticipants may have an inadequate frame of reference for assessing the effort required to complete adult literacy programs. After all, if it takes a year to advance one grade in school full time, how much will it take to advance one grade by attending an adult literacy program four hours a week? The perceived answer, as inaccurate as it might be, may magnify the perception of effort.

Perceived effort, however, is not limited to the effort involved in learning. It includes the effort needed to overcome structural obstacles such as locating child care and finding out more about the program prior to enrollment. When all is said and done, and all the things which must be accomplished to complete an adult literacy program are tallied, it is no wonder that nonparticipants think twice.

Situational Barriers

Virtually every study from Johnstone and Rivera (1965) to the Iowa Nonparticipation Study (Beder, 1989a, 1990a) has noted that situational barriers are a factor in nonparticipation. Indeed, the prevalence of situational barriers is one of the factors which separates adult education from preadult education. Its importance stems from the fact that, unlike children, adults must allocate their resources between many "mandatory" activities nested in the family, work, and community. Studies conducted on literate adult populations have found that economic cost and time are typically the greatest situational barriers to continued education but, perhaps because it is "free," time related situational barriers seem to have a greater impact on adult literacy education than economic cost.

For nonparticipants in adult literacy, the two most important sources of situational barriers are time conflicts generated by the family and by work, although transportation can be an issue for

some. Family and work are the two greatest arenas of adult responsibilities. Thus, when the time needed to care for a family or when
time on the job conflict with adult literacy education, it is quite
understandable that education will take second place.

Time might be less of a problem were the family lives and work
lives of low literates routine and were protracted participation not
required for success. If such were the case, learners could budget
scarce time without fear that it would be encroached upon. Unfortunately this is not the case. When a child is sick, when a part time
job is needed temporarily to keep the family solvent, and when one's
job requires overtime it is extremely difficult to attend adult literacy
classes which meet the same times each week. In belief that they can
not keep to the schedule, many low literates stay home. After all,
they ask, why start something you do not believe you can finish?

Dislike for School

As we have seen from the discussion of nonparticipation in
literate populations, negative attitudes toward adult education are
a common factor in nonparticipation. They pertain to perceptions
about lack of quality (Scanlan & Darkenwald, 1984), lack of course
relevance (Darkenwald & Valentine, 1985; Martindale & Drake,
1989) and the irrelevance of education to professional practice (Blais,
Duquette & Painchaud, 1989). Yet when applied to the low literate
population these negative attitudes seem to pertain to school itself—
and to all the things associated with it (Hayes, 1988; Beder, 1989a,
1990a; Quigley, 1989).

In understanding these attitudes, it is critical to examine how
they are produced and to what they precisely pertain. It is quite
likely that for such an understanding we have to focus on previous
experience with schooling. From the Iowa Studies and the qualitative research of such authors as Fingeret (1985) and Mezirow, Darkenwald, and Knox (1975), it is possible to identify two groups. The
first is comprised of low literates who failed to complete school for
lack of opportunity, individuals who were forced to leave in order
to work or because further schooling was not available. In rural Iowa
during the depression, for example, large numbers of elementary
school students could not attend high school simply because there
were no high schools in rural areas and because their families lacked
the resources to send them to schools in the large towns and cities.

For many of the "lack of opportunity" group, school was a pleasant experience, and their attitudes toward it remain positive.

This group, however, is an older group; secondary schooling today is nearly universally available. For the second group, which is younger, school was a contested terrain. For many there were major discontinuities between their cultural behaviors and attitudes and those of the school, discontinuities which bred conflict and rebellion—sometimes overt, sometimes silent. Since the values of the schools were not the values of their own cultural experience, they failed to produce the behaviors the schools expected and were thus labeled stupid, uncooperative, and incorrigible. For those of the second group, leaving school was almost a self-fulfilling prophecy and few mourned their passing.

It is not difficult to understand why members of the second group, those who opposed school and were in turn opposed, retain their dislike for the institution during adulthood. If there is hope, it lies with an understanding of the object of dislike. Those who dislike school do not necessarily dislike education or learning. Rather, the object of dislike seems to be the institution and all its trappings and they fear that "going back to adult classes would be like going to high school all over again" (Beder & Quigley, 1990).

Clearly, a dislike for school can only be ameliorated by a de-schooling of adult literacy education, by developing programs which lack the material and symbolic elements of previous schooling which are so distasteful. To some extent this seems to have happened. Fingeret (1985), for example, notes that teachers take a highly non-authoritarian stance towards adult literacy learners to the point, unfortunately, of condescension. Yet a nonauthoritarian stance is not likely to have great impact on nonparticipants who perceive the school to be a symbolic place and never experience the "warmth" of an adult literacy classroom.

Dealing With Nonparticipation

There has been considerable discussion in adult literacy education of a demand population (Developmental Associates, 1980), a sort of "triage" approach which argues that resources should be targeted towards those who are most likely to attend. This approach makes sense when one realizes that adult literacy resources are limited and are most efficiently allocated to those who are most likely to attend and persist. Furthermore, focusing on the demand population requires few alterations of the present system which is currently successful in reaching about 8% of the target population as defined by the Adult Education Act. And given the reasons for nonparticipation in adult literacy, it is difficult to see how participation in the current system can be significantly extended to the great masses of low literate adults, and thus the social impact of adult literacy is limited.

For those masses of low literates who do not perceive a need for adult literacy it is attractive to assume that since they are autonomous adults in a free society, the choice is theirs. But what about the social costs of their nonparticipation and what if they have been socially conditioned to lack the need by an unequal society? There are at least two ways they might be reached. First, adult literacy might be more closely associated with things these adults do need. Rather than being conceived as an end in itself, literacy education would become part of programs targeted towards different, more valued ends. But what might these different ends be, and to what extent would current adult literacy teaching-learning technologies "fit" the situation? We do not have the answers. Second, we might attempt to alter the low perception of need through stimulational advertising, to create through promotion a need which does not now exist. To do so, however, would be extremely expensive, and even then success would not be insured.

Dealing with perceived effort is likewise difficult, for not only must we deal with the actual effort the endeavor requires, but we must deal with the perception of that effort as well. First we must determine how the learners' actual effort can be reduced. Clearly, learning centers which allow learners to proceed at their own pace according to their own schedules are a step in the right direction, but a relatively large concentration of learners is needed to sustain a learning center and this rules out the approach in many locales. Establishing incremental, tangible benchmarks for progress might also help so that enroute to their ultimate goal students would realize that they are getting somewhere. Yet none of these solutions deals with the *perception* of effort.

The perception of effort, like dislike for school, stems from its reference point—school. The link between school and nonparticipation has to be recognized, as nonparticipation is not merely an adult literacy phenomenon; it is a phenomenon nested in the entire educational system. It may well be that prior experience with schooling is the single most potent factor in discriminating those who attend adult literacy programs from those who do not, and it may be the most difficult to treat as attitudes toward school are deep seated. How can adult literacy education be separated from a *school* context? Certainly we need to better understand the symbolic aspects of school and its trappings such as buildings, teachers, classes, and instructional materials. We also need to better understand how attitudes toward school are formed and to then link school reform with adult literacy program reform. To the extent that attitudes toward school are vested in previously unproductive role relationships between students and school officials, we need to redefine both student and teacher in adult literacy education so that a student is not simply the material object of teachers' well meaning actions. In short, substantial reform of adult literacy education may be necessary if those who are forced out of school are not to remain part of the low literate, nonparticipant population.

Given the basic logic of participation presented in the opening paragraphs of this chapter, it is possible to conclude that nonparticipation in adult literacy education stems from two kinds of factors: factors which suppress motivation such as low perception of need, perceived effort, and dislike for school, and situational factors which serve as barriers to those whose demand for adult literacy education is positive. Unlike motivational factors, situational factors affect both participants and nonparticipant populations, and an increase in participation is likely for both groups if they are removed. The treatment is obviously better sophistication in program planning so that the constraints which derive from life conflicts are not abetted by poor scheduling and program access.

Finally, nonparticipation in adult literacy education is part of the larger phenomenon of nonparticipation in adult education. Indeed, many of the factors which constrain participation at all levels have their parallels in adult literacy education. Yet nonparticipation in adult literacy is also strongly affected by its context, a context which has experiential roots in previous schooling, a context in which learning requires substantial sacrifices over time, and a context in which literacy may be more valued by society than by its intended recipients.

CHAPTER 5

Outcomes and Impact

Up to this point in this volume adult literacy education has been defined and described. Why those eligible for adult literacy education participate and why they do not has also been discussed. A critical issue remains, however, and it relates to the results of participation in adult literacy education. Does participation in adult literacy education make a difference, and if so, what difference? We will begin to answer this question by focusing on the federal adult literacy program and will conclude with a discussion of community based programs.

THE FEDERAL PROGRAM

As noted previously, the federal program is the largest component of the adult literacy enterprise in the United States, and in 1988 served 3 million students (Pugsley, 1990). The federal program is subsidized by funds authorized by the Adult Education Act, funds which are supplemented by state allocations in most locales. At the state level, the federal program is administered by state education agencies, which, in the great majority of cases, are the same agencies that administer the public schools. The term ABE (adult basic education) is often used to refer to the federal program, although ABE has other connotations as well.

The analysis of the federal program presented here is based on eight comprehensive impact studies chosen because they are among the most reputable and because they span a number of years. However, it is important at the outset to discuss the limitations of

99

this research. The most serious limitation is that even the most am-
bitious impact studies lack adequate controls. The basic problem is
simply this: To assess impact in a truly convincing manner, the research must show that adult literacy education *causes* the impact
noted. To do this the research methodology must control for any
factors which could interfere with or bias the results. The most de-
fensible way of accomplishing this is to employ an experimental
design in which those who are eligible for adult literacy are randomly assigned to two groups, one which receives instruction and
one which does not. Impact is then measured in both groups after
an appropriate period of time, and the two groups are compared on
the impact variables. Unfortunately, however, it is nearly impossible
to implement such a design on a large scale basis in the real world.
In fact, only one of the eight studies discussed here has included a
"control group" of nonparticipants for the purpose of comparison,
and in this study there was no random assignment of study participants.

Lack of experimental controls confounds and limits the validity of research findings. For example, as we will see, nearly all
impact studies show a positive effect on students' employment. Yet
in the absence of experimental controls, it is impossible to know
whether increased employment is due to participation in the program or to other causes such as a general increase in employment
among the target population. Impacts could also be due to the fact
that adult literacy students are a select population who would have
increased their employment even without attending adult literacy.
After all, by the very act of enrolling in adult literacy education,
students demonstrate many of the traits which promote successful
employment, traits such as motivation and the desire to succeed.

All the studies reviewed here are based on survey research and
this produces two other limitations. First, most surveys measure
learners' perceptions of impact rather than objective impact. For
example, based on their perceptions, survey respondents may report
that their children do better in school as a consequence of parents'
attending adult literacy education but, in the absence of objective
measures such as actual grades, it is difficult to know whether the
perceptions are accurate. Neither can it be known whether respondents have supplied us with the truth as they perceive it or with answers which are merely socially acceptable. Second, the response
rates for the different studies vary considerably, and some are quite

low. It may be that those who benefit the most are the most likely to respond to impact surveys and, if this were so, impact findings would obviously be inflated.

Imperfection need not lead to despair, however. We can have considerable confidence in the prevalence of an impact if a number of studies conducted over a number of years yield the same conclusion. Thus the credibility of claiming a particular impact comes not only from the quality of a specific study, but also from the comparison of findings from several studies. Yet although such comparisons are important, for two reasons they are not easy. First, different impact studies include different variables, and even when variables are the same the questions which elicit them are phrased differently from study to study. Second, studies use different time periods for assessing impact, and this obviously affects the magnitude of the impact reported. Quite obviously, the ability to deal with the issue of impact depends also on the quality of the studies reviewed. Consequently, before specific impacts are discussed, a description of the studies is needed.

Eight Studies

The eight studies include three national studies and state impact studies for New Jersey, Ohio, Tennessee, Maryland, and Iowa.

The System Development Corporation Study

The first national impact study of the federal program was commissioned by the federal government under contract to the System Development Corporation. It was conducted in 1971 and authored by Kent (Kent, 1973). Desiring to focus on what was then the priority population for the program, the study excluded enrollees over age 44, as well as students in English as a second language and GED preparation classes, institutional enrollees, and migrants. Sampling began with the selection of a random stratified sample of 15 states. Selected states were then asked to supply enrollment data, usually by county or school district. Enrollments were then divided geographically into six segments of equal size, and a program was randomly drawn from each segment. Finally, from each program three classes were randomly selected in a way which yielded about 25 students per class, and teachers provided class rosters and attendance data. The final sample yielded 92 programs, 206 classes, and 2,318 students.

Two instruments were used in the study, the Test of Adult Basic Education (TABE) to measure learning gain and an interview survey to collect other impact data. Students were tested with the TABE twice at four month intervals. The number of students who took the first TABE test was 1,108, and 441 completed all tests for a rather poor response rate. Thus test gains may be inflated if more poorly performing students failed to take the second test—perhaps because they had dropped out.

Students were interviewed in person or by telephone three times—initially, at 12 months, and then at 18 months. The response rate for the 12 month follow up was 74% and 79% for the 18 month follow up; this response is quite respectable. Compared to many others, the System Development Corporation Study is quite solid, and considerable care was taken to insure valid results. The major weakness is, as we have mentioned, the lack of experimental controls. Student persistence, learning gain, economic impact, educational impact, and students' perceptions of their improvement were among the impact variables measured.

The Development Associates Study

In 1979, Development Associates conducted another large scale assessment of the federal adult literacy program (Developmental Associates, 1980). Although the study included several objectives which are ancillary to the issue of student impact, measurement of the benefits to participants and to society were a major part of the endeavor. Data was collected from teachers and students. To obtain it, site visits were made to a probability sample of 111 local programs stratified by type of program and size of federal grant. This yielded information from 434 teachers and 3,115 students.

Desiring to gather data on students who had dropped out from the program, the sampling frame for the student impact portion of the study was developed from lists supplied by teachers of students who had enrolled in the semester prior to the site visit. However, from the 3,061 names supplied, only 1,177 could be contacted for a relatively disappointing response rate of 38.5%. Furthermore, in respect to gender, race, age, and residence, those who were interviewed were found to differ substantially from those who could not be reached. Thus, although the sampling procedures of the Developmental Associates Study were acceptable, the response bias undermines the validity of the student impact data. Impact variables included student persistence, attainment of personal goals, self-concept, gains in basic skills, family relationships, life skills, and job acquisition.

Federal Data

The most current data on impacts and results of literacy education comes from data collected by the Office of Vocational and Adult Education of the United States Department of Education as part of its monitoring responsibility. This data is supplied to the federal government by the various states which compile it from information supplied by local programs. Clearly, the validity of the data is conditional on the accuracy of local data gathering and reporting. As a validity check, data supplied by each state is analyzed by a computer program which assesses whether it makes sense given a state's demographic characteristics. If the data is deemed questionable, the state is deleted from the compilation. The federal data contains information on program completion rates, educational impact, and economic impact.

The New Jersey Study

While national impact data may be generalized to the federal program as a whole, given the noted limitations, of course, the results of statewide studies can not be generalized beyond their boundaries. Nevertheless, these studies permit elaboration and refinement of outcomes and impact. One of the best state studies was conducted in New Jersey in 1983 (Darkenwald & Valentine, 1984). The New Jersey study had two objectives pertinent to our discussion: to assess the outcomes and impact of participation in ABE and GED preparation and to determine the benefits which accrue to adult secondary education students who receive their diplomas.

The outcomes and impacts portion of the study employed a random sample proportionate to size procedure which resulted in a representative sample of 400 students in nine separate programs. English as a second language students were excluded from the study as were institutionalized adults. Data was collected seven to eight months after program enrollment using a follow up survey. Items for the survey were generated by reviewing previous impact research and by conducting brainstorming sessions with teachers and administrators. Purposefully, the survey included a large number of open ended questions that were later inductively coded by the researchers. Subjects were interviewed via telephone with a very respectable response rate of 74%.

The sample for the high school completion benefits portion of the study included 300 randomly selected GED graduates who had participated in adult literacy instruction and 200 adults who had graduated from board of education diploma programs in five of the nine study programs. Data was collected by means of a one page mailed questionnaire with a response rate of 50%.

The New Jersey study was carefully designed and executed, but it too suffers from a lack of experimental controls. A positive feature of this study is its use of open ended questions. Obviously a study can only determine what its questions ask. If respondents are presented with a highly structured, narrow range of response options, their answers are limited to those options. Although the analysis of open ended questions is quite time consuming, a much wider range of response is possible and information which might otherwise be lost is included. The New Jersey study measured economic impact, educational impact, basic skills improvement, student persistence, attainment of personal goals, affective impact, and impact on children.

The Ohio Study

The Ohio impact study, reported by Boggs, Buss, and Yarnell (1979), was conducted in 1977 and measured six areas of impact: impact on social involvement, on employment, on children, on voting, on home ownership, and on education. The study collected data from two different groups, a group of former students and a comparison group of adults who were eligible for adult literacy education, but who had not participated. To identify a sample of former students, the Ohio study employed a multistage random sampling design which resulted in 12 programs being selected that together accounted for 3,500 former students. Data was collected through a telephone survey. However, valid phone numbers and/or addresses could be obtained for only 1,200 former students and interviews were completed for only 351. The comparison group of adults who were eligible for ABE but had not participated was identified through a similar multistage random design. This resulted in over 90,000 telephone calls being made to achieve 1,536 completed interviews.

Although the Ohio study is one of the few impact studies to include a comparison group, since there was no random assignment to treatment and control groups it is impossible to determine whether or not differences between the groups were due to participation in ABE or to other unknown factors. In fact, considerable selection bias is quite likely. In addition, the low response rate for the former ABE students raises the probability of some response bias.

The Tennessee Study

The Tennessee study was conducted by Jones and Petry (1980) of Memphis State University. Among several objectives the study sought to measure students' perceptions of their educational experience. As in other impact research, the study employed a survey which in this case had two parts. The first part, which is of primary concern here, was comprised of outcome variables descriptive of quality of life. The second measured student perceptions of classroom relationships.

Development of the quality of life component began with a search of the literature for relevant variables. Initially, 50 variables were selected and organized into seven categories by a panel of six raters. The impact categories were self-expression, self-concept, family life, life in general, leisure, relationships with others, and relationships to society. Through the rating process, the list of 50 variables was reduced to 35, and, following a pilot test, the list was further reduced to 26.

The sample for the study was identified by selecting 89 programs. In each, supervisors selected 25 students and administered the survey to them personally. This provided a potential sample of 2,225 students. Surveys were returned from 72 of the 89 programs resulting in 1,623 usable responses and a response rate of 73%. Rather than measuring impact through a follow up analysis as with most other studies, the study used length of time in the program as its independent variable. The Tennessee study differs from others in that it defines impact in terms of quality of life. It, like others, lacks experimental controls and fails to report the reliability of its quality of life scales.

The Maryland Study

The Maryland study, conducted by Walker, Ewert, and Whaples (1981), employed personal interviews to gather data with a survey developed from previous impact studies and discussions with ABE/GED students, teachers, and administrators. The sample was developed by randomly selecting 26 ABE/GED classes stratified by the number of classes offered by each county. From each class, five students were selected—randomly in most cases, but not in all. From a potential 130 cases, 116 usable responses were obtained for a very respectable response rate of 88%. Impact variables included economic impact, basic skill acquisition, social involvement, attitudinal change, and personal relationships. The Maryland study measured perceptions of impact. Respondents, who were all current students, were asked whether they perceived that they had benefited, without controlling for the length of time they had been in the program. This flaw may have suppressed the amount of impact found, as many of those interviewed may not have participated long enough for an impact to register.

The Iowa Study

The Iowa impact study (Beder & Valentine, 1987) was part of a larger effort designed to ascertain learners' motivations for attending a literacy program and to segment the population into groups which represented the behavioral structure of the population. The primary sample was developed using a random proportionate to size design similar to that of the New Jersey study. From 255 Iowa classes and 3,090 students, 323 students were selected who had completed less than 11 grades of previous schooling. English as a second language and institutionalized students were excluded. From the primary sample, 109 students were randomly selected for a follow up study which was conducted through telephone interviews six months after initial data collection. The response rate was excellent—91%. In addition, each student's teacher was surveyed regarding the student's progress and the response rate for teachers was 100%. Impact variables included student satisfaction, life improvement, teachers' assessment of progress, and persistence in the program. While high response rates and careful sampling are strengths of the Iowa study, the number of impact variables included is limited.

Impact of the Federal Program

Based on the eight studies, the impact of the federal program can be addressed in five different areas: impact on human capital, impact on basic skill gain, social impact, impact on the attainment of students' personal goals, and affective impact.

Human Capital

As repeatedly noted, human capital theory provides a fundamental justification for the federal program. The basic argument is that education promotes worker productivity which in turn results in national productivity and increased national wealth. Since there is more national wealth to be shared, everyone benefits. Since everyone benefits from investments in adult literacy education, tax payers are willing to subsidize the program. Conversely, however, if there were no positive impact on human capital, and the benefits of adult literacy education accrued solely to individual students, public subsidy would not be warranted.

Rightfully or wrongfully, demonstrating impact on human capital is critical to the survival of the federal adult literacy effort. There are four components to human capital impact: increased employment and increased quality of employment, increased income, reduced need for public assistance, and continued investments by students in further education. Clearly, unemployed adults are not economically productive. Increases in job quality are important, because productivity is strongly abetted by technology and job quality is associated with workers' ability to master complex technologies. Increases in income demonstrate that the investment in adult literacy education is indeed creating national wealth and an improved tax base. Similarly, when the incidence of public assistance is reduced, a major source of expensive transfer payments to the poor is reduced, and if those who complete basic education continue their educations, their capacity to produce is further enhanced.

Increased Employment and Job Quality. In respect to employment and job quality, Kent (1973) found that over a period of 18 months employment increased among adult literacy students from 55% to 65% and that the number of those reporting some job related earnings rose from 58% to 70%. Development Associates (1980), however, reports that only 18% of the ABE students believed that participating helped them to get a better job, and that only a small number had enrolled to get a job (8%) or to get a better job (6%). The government (Pugsley, 1990) reports that in 1988, a total of 12% of the participants obtained a job and that 8% obtained better jobs.

Turning to state studies, the New Jersey Study found that 18 months after obtaining a high school diploma, 58% of the students who were initially unemployed obtained jobs, a figure which is offset by 15% of the sample who initially held jobs but lost them. In addition, 45% of those who were initially employed reported that they had obtained better jobs, 29% had received promotions; 78% believed that they were more likely to keep their jobs, and 76% reported that they were able to do their jobs better.

The follow up component of the New Jersey study found that after seven to eight months there was a net gain in employment of 13%; 18% of the sample changed jobs and for 61% the change resulted in a better job. In addition, 42% obtained a raise; 65% felt that their job performance had improved; 14% had been promoted; 57% felt that their job security had improved. Of those who were unemployed, 79% believed that adult literacy education would help them find a better job. Echoing the Development Associates study, however, the New Jersey study found that only a minority (20%) of the adult literacy students enrolled either to acquire a job or to acquire a better job.

The Maryland study reports that 85% of their research subjects perceived adult literacy education would help them acquire jobs; two thirds thought that their chances of getting a raise would improve, and 63% felt that as a consequence of adult literacy education they were able to do their jobs better. The Iowa study reports that at the six month follow-up, 77% of the students believed that their lives had improved because of attending adult literacy education. However, only 9% attributed this improvement to job acquisition or improvement. Finally, the Ohio study found that former ABE students were more likely to be employed, promoted, and secure in their jobs than adults who were eligible for ABE but had not participated.

Increased Income. Only three of the eight studies deal directly with income as an impact variable, and this is rather surprising given the importance of income to the human capital argument. Kent (1973) found a 20% gain in income over 18 months; inflation and wage fluctuations were estimated to account for 5.5% of the increase. The New Jersey study found that 93% of the those surveyed 18 months after receiving their GED or adult high school diplomas reported increases in earnings. Although the Maryland study did not measure actual income, the study did find that two thirds of the sample believed that participation in adult literacy education would help them increase their incomes.

Reduced Need for Public Assistance. Although participation in the federal adult literacy education program does seem to reduce the incidence of public assistance, the effects are small. Kent (1973) found a 4.6% reduction in those who received public assistance in an 18 month follow up, and government data for 1988 reports that 7% of the participants were removed from public welfare. The New Jersey study reports that while 26% of their sample were initially on welfare, at follow up the amount of welfare received was the same for two thirds of the welfare recipients. Eighteen percent reported that, for them, the amount of welfare had decreased, and 15% claimed that it had been eliminated. The researchers asked those whose welfare had been reduced for the reason. Forty-four percent mentioned obtaining a job; 9% mentioned making more money, and 49% reported "something else." Regarding the large "something else" response, the authors state, "It seems probable that the 'something else' answer, in large part, reflected cutbacks in benefits and a tightening of eligibility requirements at the time research was conducted" (p. 81).

Continued Further Education. Further education seems to be one of the most important human capital benefits. For example, 61% of Kent's (1973) sample expected to attend college, and 58% of Development Associates' sample planned to continue their educations. Government data for 1988 (Office of Vocational and Adult Education, 1989) reports that 201,270 of the 3 million participants entered another education or training program. The New Jersey study reports that 14 to 18 months after receiving a high school diploma, 29% of the adult literacy students had entered college, and 31% had enrolled in vocational programs. When asked whether they planned to enroll in further education, 63% of the adult literacy students who were followed up claimed that they planned to continue their educations. The impact of adult literacy education on continued education is corroborated by the Ohio study which found that adult literacy students were significantly more likely to enroll in further education than adults who were eligible for adult literacy education but who had not participated. Finally, of the 77% of the adult literacy students who noted that their lives had improved at a six month followup, 8% of the Iowa study respondents attributed the improvement to their continued education.

Discussion. Does adult literacy education have a positive effect on human capital variables? Although our eight studies generally indicate that it does, it is not all that simple. Although it seems clear that adult literacy education students do better on human capital indicators, without experimental controls there is no way to prove that adult literacy education causes human capital gains. Most certainly the state of the economy has a powerful intervening effect. For example, although the New Jersey study reports large increases in employment, the study was conducted at a time when the state was emerging from a deep recession and employment in general was on the rise. Given the economic upturn, would students have obtained jobs even without adult literacy? We do not know. Similarly, it seems likely that welfare policy coupled with the state of the economy has a much greater impact on the incidence of public assistance than does adult literacy education.

Another issue relates to the length of time it takes for impact to register. For those studies that employed a follow up methodology, the time of follow up ranged from 6 to 18 months. Yet it could be that the impact of adult literacy on human capital is enormous over a lifetime while the short term effects are modest. This would be true if adult literacy education had an enabling effect—if success provides additional opportunities which, when taken, have a cumulative effect on human capital gain. The convincingly large impact of adult literacy education on further education supports such an argument.

How important is impact on human capital? Certainly it is vital to federal policy, but how important is it to students? Kent reported that less than one third of the ABE students enrolled in order to obtain a job. For Development Associates the figure was 17%; for the New Jersey study it was 20%, and for the Iowa study (Valentine, 1990), job advancement was only the seventh most important motivation for participation in ABE of 10 motivations analyzed.

Although federal policy places human capital impact at the apex of importance, students do not. This disparity leads the authors of the New Jersey study to remark, "Where, then, lies the lack of congruence between policy and program reality? First, and most obvious, is the fact that getting a job or better job is not a relevant goal for a large proportion of program participants, particularly mature adults as opposed to recent school dropouts. Second, most of the important outcomes or benefits have little to do with employment. Finally, the accelerating trend toward linking ABE directly with job training programs poses a threat to the fundamentally *educational* nature of most programs as they are presently constituted in New Jersey and the majority of other states" (p. 92).

Basic Skill Gain

Obviously, for an educational program such as adult literacy education, learning gain is an important indication of impact. Because of the difficulty associated with large scale testing, most impact studies have relied on students' self-report of learning gain, and this is an obvious weakness. Kent's study is an exception. Kent measured learning gain with the Test of Adult Basic Education (TABE) administered twice at an interval of four months. The average gain in reading was half a grade and three tenths of a grade for mathematics. Twenty-six percent of the sample gained one grade or more in reading, and 19% gained one grade or more in mathematics. Although these gains appear to be laudable, less than half of the students took both tests, and if better students were more likely to complete both tests, the scores are inflated. Development Associates reported that 75% of their sample report gains in reading; 69% noted gains in mathematics, and 66% claimed gains in writing.

State studies show similar performance. The New Jersey study reports that 83% of its sample perceived that they could read better as a result of adult literacy education, and two thirds had used their increased reading skills to do something they could not do before, such as read newspapers. Sixty-three percent of the adult literacy students believed they could write better, but only half reported that they had used their newly acquired writing skills out of the classroom. Fifty-eight percent of the respondents claimed that their math skills had increased.

The Ohio study found that math and reading test scores were positively related to the number of hours students spent in the program, and the Maryland study reports that 76% of its sample believed they could read better as a consequence of attending the program; 81% believed that their writing had improved, and 90%

felt that their computational skills had improved. The Iowa study found that 42% of the teachers rated their students' progress as being above average in reading. The comparable figure for mathematics was 38%. Additionally, the Iowa study found that teachers' assessments of progress correlated significantly with students' tested achievement as measured by the Woodcock-Johnson Achievement Test.

It seems clear then that students do gain literacy skills as a result of participating in the federal adult literacy program. This is to be expected. However, the real issue is how much do students gain and how much gain is acceptable. There is no standard. It also seems likely that learning gain is differential, that some types of students are more likely to gain than others. The Ohio study, for example, shows a significant relationship between high reading and mathematics scores and income. Similarly, Kent reports that gains in TABE scores were influenced by reading level and gender.

Social Impact

Although the economic benefits of adult literacy education are central to the human capital justification of social impact, noneconomic aspects are also critically important to the health of society. Clearly, for a society to be truly democratic all citizens must participate, not only in the political process, but in important social institutions as well. The family may well be the most important social institution of all; it is the most basic social unit, and its success has a large impact on future generations. If adult literacy education were found to have a positive impact on social participation in general and on family relationships in specific, a strong rationale for the program would be provided.

Focusing on family impact, Kent found that 55% of his sample helped their children with homework, and this increased to 58% at a one year follow up. In a similar vein, Developmental Associates report that 51% of the students sampled claimed that better family relations were an outcome of participating in adult literacy education, and the Ohio study found that former ABE students were significantly more likely to attend their children's school meetings than nonparticipants eligible for the program. The results of the Maryland study are corroborative. Eighty-six percent of the sample who had children reported that their children requested help with homework, and 61% reported that participation in adult literacy education had increased their confidence to assist. Slightly over half of the Maryland sample felt more confident in parent-student conferences as a result of participation.

The New Jersey study provides what may be the most detailed account of family impact. The portion of the study that dealt with adult literacy graduates found that 96% of them believed that they set a better example for their children. Likewise, the follow up portion of the study which focused on current ABE students reported major family impact. Three quarters of the sample reported that they helped children more with homework; 81% talked to children more about school; 73% believed that their children had developed a better attitude toward school, and three quarters believed that their children were getting better grades as a result of the parent's participation in adult literacy education. Thus, although the research evidence is not extensive, it seems to reach the same conclusion; adult literacy education does impact on the family in a positive way.

The research indicates a positive impact for other forms of social participation as well. Although the Maryland study is limited to the perceptions of current students, it found that 50% of its sample had used the library recently; 35% claimed that participation had increased their interest in politics, and 58% reported an increased awareness of social services. Similarly, the Ohio study reported that former ABE students were more likely to use the library, access social services, engage in community activity, and register to vote than nonparticipants who were eligible for the program. Although the Ohio study found no significant relationships for voting, the New Jersey study found that 65% of the adult literacy graduates believed they knew more about how the government works.

The Tennessee study included five measures related to social impact: family life, life in general, leisure, relationships with other, and relationships with society. Significant relationships were found between hours in the program and all social impact variables.

Students' Personal Goals

Because the federal program is subsidized from tax dollars, many of its stated goals are social goals—goals which, when obtained, benefit society in general. Human capital, basic skill attainment, and social benefits fall into this category. Yet students have their own goals, and those goals are not always congruent with

society's. That students believe that they can attain their own goals
—and do—is critically important, however, for it is personal goal
attainment that motivates participation. Thus the federally supported adult literacy program must have dual impact. It must impact
on social goals if it is to retain public support, and it must impact
on students' goals if it is to attract learners.

What are the major goals for adult literacy students? Without
exception the studies show that the most important goal is attainment of high school certification, usually the GED. This seems to
be true for students at all levels, and it is hardly surprising given that
education is the mission of the program. Government data shows
that 31% of the participants in 1988 obtained high school certification (Pugsley, 1990). High school certification, however, is rarely
an end in itself and students report other goals as well.

Kent found that the main reason for attending was job advancement for 31% of the sample and that the things students most
wanted to learn were reading (48%) and working with numbers
(46%). Writing took a distant third (6%). Similarly, Development
Associates found that about one third of the students enrolled to
gain basic reading, writing, and mathematics skills. One of the
weaknesses of many studies which probe students goals, including
the two studies reported above, is that they use forced choice formats
that restrict responses to the choices provided. The New Jersey study
used an open format, however. It found that, as with other studies,
the most commonly voiced goal was to obtain a diploma (44%).
Next in importance were obtaining a job (19%) and improving basic
skills (19%). The Maryland study found that goals are related to
age. While the young generally wished to obtain the GED for vocational reasons, 28% of those between 31 and 40 years of age
desired the certification so that they could continue their educations. For the Iowa study, which like the New Jersey study employed
a open response format, GED acquisition was again the most important student goal (64%). Obtaining general reading and writing
skills took second place (12%).

Do students believe that they are achieving their goals? The
answer is a cautioned "yes." The caveat comes from the fact that
many studies did not include program dropouts in their samples or
that the studies underrepresented these dropouts; it would be expected that students who were unable to meet their goals through

the program would be less likely to persist. Kent found that after a year in the program 81% believed that they had progressed in reading, 74% noted progress in computational skills, but only 65% felt that their writing had improved. Development Associates report that 43% of their sample believed they had attained their goals, and 38% felt they were making progress.

At the end of a seven month period, the New Jersey study found that 13% of the follow up sample believed they had totally reached their goals, and 49% believed they had made considerable progress. About one quarter of the New Jersey sample had passed the GED exam after seven months. The Maryland study reports that students perceived that they were meeting their basic skill goals through the program. Seventy-six percent felt they could read better; 81% believed they could write better, and 90% perceived their computational skills had improved. The findings of the Iowa study are similar. At the six month follow up, 43% of the teachers reported that their students were making above average progress toward meeting their own goals, and one third were making average progress.

It seems clear from the available evidence that students are able to attain personal goals through the federal adult literacy program. However, the significance of personal impact is clouded by the general exclusion or underrepresentation of dropouts in the research. There is an old adage among adult educators: the disenchanted vote with their feet. Those whose goals were not met may not have been present for the counting.

Affective Impact

The impact of adult literacy education comes from the changes it produces in learners. Although impacts are often instrumental, such as increases in employment or income, they can also be internal, pertaining to such things as changes in feelings or attitudes. The most commonly researched affective impact is self-concept, and all studies reported here show increases in this area. For the students studied by Development Associates, improved self-concept was the most prevalent outcome; 84% believed their self-concepts had improved. Similarly, 92% of the New Jersey sample noted that they felt better about themselves as a result of attending adult literacy education. When the researchers asked why, two thirds mentioned

personal accomplishment or academic achievement, and only 11%
mentioned increased economic or educational opportunity. In the
Ohio study, the self-confidence of former ABE students was found
to be significantly higher than that of those who were eligible for
ABE but had never participated. Likewise, 89% of the Maryland
students believed that participation in the program increased their
self-confidence, and the Tennessee study reported that increased
self-concept was highly associated with the length of time students
had participated in the program. When students in Iowa who had
indicated that their lives had improved as a result of ABE were asked
why, by far the most common reason given was increased self-confidence.

The data on self-concept is quite convincing and supports a
conclusion that increased self-concept is the most universal impact
of the federal adult literacy program. This is interesting for two
reasons. First, improvement in self-concept is not a stated goal of
the federal program. In fact, one wonders if the public would continue to support federal subsidy of the program if this were the only
impact. Second, improved self-concept may be a particularly significant outcome because of its enabling power. There is a wealth of
research which demonstrates that a positive self-concept enhances
performance in a wide array of life endeavors, and it may be that
the enabling effect enhances many aspects of students' lives.

COMMUNITY BASED PROGRAMS

As noted in the first chapter, although some community based
adult literacy programs are funded in part by federal and state allocations, most differ substantially from traditional ABE. For community based programs, learning to read and write is viewed as the
means to some other end such as personal empowerment or community and economic development. Many favor group oriented instructional methods over individual based methods; classes are not
generally conducted in public schools, and students usually come
from the hardest to reach segments of the target population (Association for Community Based Education, 1986a). In addition,
many community based literacy programs take an emancipatory

literacy approach directed more toward social change than to individual development.

Amidst a general lack of impact data for community based literacy programs, there is one exception, and that is the Association for Community Based Education's (ACBE) evaluation of 1988–89 (Association for Community Based Education, 1989). ACBE's sample of programs was basically a convenience sample of community based literacy programs that volunteered to be evaluated in promise of $8,000 minigrants for each. Nine programs were ultimately included in the evaluation.

Ten outcomes were selected for measurement, and programs were permitted to select the outcomes that they were to be evaluated on. Outcomes included reading skills, writing skills, math skills, oral language skills, reading activities outside of class, writing activities outside of class, fostering children's intellectual and academic development, community activities and contribution, self-esteem, and self-determination. Data was collected initially, at eight weeks, and finally at six to seven months.

Six programs chose to evaluate reading. For low level readers, reading skills were measured by the SRA Reading Index, and for intermediate readers the Adult Basic Learning Exam (ABLE) was used. Three of the six programs showed significant gains in reading, and for two of the three the gains were large. Five programs chose to evaluate writing which was measured by the CAT Writing Assessment System. Only one program showed a significant increase in writing. Similarly, one of the two programs that selected to evaluate math skills as measured by the ABLE exhibited a significant gain.

Results were mixed for the evaluation of reading and writing out of class, and the results were held to be questionable because of instrumentation problems. A low number of research subjects precluded solid conclusions regarding the effect of adult literacy education on the intellectual and academic development of students' children.

Up to this point, the ACBE evaluation appears to be quite traditional, as indeed it was since a purpose of the evaluation was to demonstrate the credibility of community based literacy to "a wide range of people concerned with adult literacy" and to help programs prepare submissions to the Department of Education's

Program Effectiveness Panel. Results, therefore, may have been distorted by the use of traditional measures for nontraditional programs. The evaluation did, however, include three outcomes which have particular relevance to community based programs: information on learners' community activities and contributions, self-esteem, and self-determination.

Community activities and contributions were measured by an instrument developed by the researchers which probed fourteen kinds of activities and contributions. Both programs in which this dimension was measured showed significant gains. Using the Culture-Free Self Esteem Inventory, self-esteem was measured for all nine programs and seven showed significant gains. Self-determination, measured by an instrument that asked twenty questions regarding self-direction, planning, initiative, persistence, and success, was measured for seven programs, three of which showed significant gains. For one program the gain was large and cumulative.

There seem to be several important lessons from the ACBE evaluation. First, programs varied widely in the criteria they chose to be evaluated with and in the impacts recorded. This may reflect the fact that different aspects of literacy may be emphasized differentially by programs in accordance with their particular goals and clientele. Second, on the standard measures of impact, such as reading and mathematics gain, community based programs compare favorably with traditional ABE programs. Finally, we still need to know a great deal more about impact in the areas that community based programs emphasize the most—the impact of literacy on learner self-affirmation, for example, and the impact on collective social action within the community.

Does adult literacy education have a positive impact on both learners and society? While the absolute validity of even the best research on the question is limited, together the various impact studies present a preponderance of evidence to the affirmative. Yet there are still many unanswered questions, and first and foremost among them may be the issue of impact itself. To date, only direct impact has been studied in a large scale study, and the longest period of follow up in a national impact study has been 18 months (Kent, 1973). It may well be, however, that the most important impacts are cumulative, indirect, and long term. For example, earning a GED may enable some to continue on to higher education. Once they have earned bachelor's degrees, they may obtain lucrative employment. Having higher incomes, they may decide to invest in the education of their children who then benefit indirectly from their parent's acquired literacy. Are this scenario and others like it realistic? Are the most important impacts of adult literacy cumulative, indirect, and long term? We do not know, and only a well-designed longitudinal study can provide the answer.

CHAPTER 6

Implications for Policy and Practice

The purpose of this chapter is to utilize the findings of the research reported in chapters one through five to raise issues that have implications for policy and practice in adult literacy education. As noted in the first chapter, four basic questions will be addressed: What should the goals and purposes of adult literacy education be? Who should be served? How can learners best be attracted? How can adult literacy education best be provided? Clearly, these questions are interrelated and cannot be considered in isolation from each other. Just as clearly, a resolution of the issues raised by these questions depends as much on values, attitudes, and ideologies as it does on the guidance which empirical research can provide. These questions have been discussed before as they related to the various studies; indeed, they are fundamental to a coherent adult literacy policy. Yet ramifications and nuances have not always been made plain in the debates surrounding these questions, and the discussion of these issues has at times been confused and chaotic. Hopefully this analysis will move the discussion forward.

GOALS AND PURPOSES

To a great extent a discussion of what the goals and purposes of adult literacy education should be depends on how adult literacy education is defined. If, for example, literacy is defined simply as the ability to read and write, it follows that the goal is to instill reading and writing skills regardless of use context. Similarly, if literacy is defined functionally as learners' ability to function within

121

a specific context, the goal becomes to teach whatever skills are needed to operate effectively within that context. Since goals are implicit in the various definitions of literacy, a discussion of goals and purposes must begin with clarity of definition. Otherwise, we are discussing different things while pretending to be discussing the same thing.

For the purposes of the discussion here, the definition of literacy proposed by Csikszentmihalyi (1990) will be used. Csikszentmihalyi defines literacy as the ability to code and decode meaning stored in symbolic form. Using this definition, the focus turns to the symbols in question and to the context of the coding and decoding activity. Traditional literacy is the ability to code and decode print within a general context. Functional literacy is the ability to code and decode the symbolic meanings embodied in a specific context, the workplace for example, and emancipatory literacy is the ability to code and decode the symbolic meanings of society itself. The issue for goals and purposes then becomes the question "on which symbolic systems should adult literacy focus and to what end?"

One might argue that print, and perhaps numbers, are the most basic symbolic systems and that we should concentrate on them because mastery of print and numbers enables learners to negotiate other symbolic systems. I, for example, have been able to master the symbols needed to operate a computer, because I am able to read computer manuals. Such an argument, however, ignores the fact that, as Freire and Macedo (1987) note, coding and decoding the *word* does not necessarily enable one to the decode the *world*. Words have different symbolic meanings for different social groups. As Willis (1978) notes, for the working class Hammertown lads "work" means manual labor for a weekly pay envelope, while for the mainstream culture which the lads resist work means a career for an annual salary. Interpreting "work" as they do, the lads are predestined for the working class culture to which they were born. The lesson is that the shared symbolic meanings of class, race, and gender are socially constructed and are part of the mechanisms which maintain inequality. It follows that although the ability to code and decode print is necessary, it may be insufficient. To free themselves from the conditions which have made them disadvantaged, the disadvantaged must also be able to decode the basic social meanings which perpetuate an unequal society.

With the previous discussion as introduction, it is possible to identify four basic ends of adult literacy education: social mobility, social change, economic productivity, and learners' attainment of their own goals.

Social Mobility

Along with economic productivity, social mobility has been one of the major presumed outcomes of federal adult literacy policy. For lack of literacy, low literates are perceived as being dependent on society and unable to reap its benefits. This is evident in the stated purpose of the Adult Education Act which begins as follows, "It is the purpose of this title to assist the States to improve educational opportunities for adults who lack the level of literacy skills requisite to effective citizenship and productive employment . . . " (PL 100–297, p. 1). According to this line of reasoning, low literates are unable to rise in the system because they lack needed skills. It is presumed that once these skills are provided social mobility will be enhanced for those who master them.

In Chapter Four it was concluded from an analysis of eight outcomes and impact studies that, in respect to socioeconomic mobility, the federal adult literacy program has been effective. Adult literacy education does seem to enhance learners' abilities to acquire better employment and to earn more. Salutary effects were also found for social participation. Yet three fundamental problems still remain. First, if adult literacy education does promote social mobility, it does so only for those who participate. However, only about 8% of the eligible target population do participate. Furthermore, by virtue of their motivation to accomplish something difficult, participants may be an upwardly mobile population to begin with, a population which might have risen in the system even without adult literacy education. Second, although adult literacy may promote social mobility for some learners, the socioeconomic status of low literates as a class seems to have been little affected by the federal adult literacy program. Indeed, while the number of adults enrolled in the federal program increased from 2 million in 1980 to 3 million in 1990 (Pugsley, 1990), during the same decade the percentage of American families below the poverty line increased from 11.4 to 12.8 (Friedrich, 1990). Thus if adult literacy education does promote social mobility, its power is surpassed considerably by other social and economic forces, many of which limit mobility. Finally, the logic of the social mobility argument defines low literates as being socially dependent human beings whose life success is problematic for lack of vital skills. This logic feeds the social stigma that society attaches to low literacy, a stigma which, in its own right, deters social mobility.

If social mobility is a valid and obtainable end for adult literacy education, then at least two things must transpire before it can be attained on a large scale. First, the adult literacy program must reach a much higher proportion of those who could benefit from it. Second, social, educational, and economic programs that are designed to promote social mobility must be coordinated at all levels, particularly at the local level. This is important, because the delivery system for adult literacy education is often fragmented and isolated, and as a consequence the social impact of adult literacy education is reduced substantially. As a New Jersey white paper notes (NJALL, 1990), "On the state level, sixty-three different programs provide funds for adult literacy education and job training. These programs are administered by more than six separate state departments, including the Departments of Education, Higher Education, Vocational Education, Labor, Human Services, and Community Affairs. The same diffusion of responsibility occurs on the county and local levels. The outcome is that limited resources, lack of coordination, and 'turf problems' are evident at every level of administration" (p. 3).

Social Change

While the federal adult literacy program is oriented primarily toward helping individual learners to function more effectively in American society, as noted many times in this volume, there are some who believe that adult literacy education should be directed toward changing the social institutions that maintain and continually reproduce society—a society which they believe is fundamentally unequal. Adult literacy education which is directed to this end has several labels which include emancipatory literacy, popular education, critical pedagogy, and radical pedagogy. Emancipatory educators, many of whom work in the community based sector, believe that low literacy is a social construction. They argue that through its social institutions—particularly the schools—society reproduces a disadvantaged, low literate underclass. This, they believe, insures that there will always be a supply of inexpensive labor to fill the least desired jobs in the economic structure. Social mobility is simply a blank promise, a carrot before the horse designed to motivate the underclass to participate in the system. It follows from this logic that if low literacy is to be eradicated the social structures and ideological belief systems which produce it must be changed, and those changes can come only from the collective action of the disadvantaged class.

Literacy in this view is but a means to an end, a set of critical coding and decoding skills which help low literates to understand the political, economic, and ideological forces which perpetuate their place in the social order. Such a critical understanding is crucial to collective empowerment and successful social action. While the traditional adult literacy system focuses on individual development, emancipatory educators focus on collective change. Learners generally have a major say in how literacy programs are conducted, and group oriented methods are favored over individual oriented methods.

The answer to the question of whether adult literacy education should be directed toward helping individuals to function in society, or whether it should be directed toward assisting groups to change the structures which create and maintain illiteracy obviously depends on one's view of the social order. The belief that the social system is good, democratic, and basically just supports traditional adult literacy practice, while a belief that the social system is unequal, undemocratic, and unjust supports the position of emancipatory literacy. It is quite possible that there is truth in both sets of beliefs, that while our society is basically democratic and just there are also pockets of severe oppression that are vested in racism or circumscribed by the boundaries of the inner city. It may also be that for those who are genuinely oppressed, emancipatory literacy is the best way out. Yet emancipatory literacy programs represent but a small minority of the available adult literacy programs, and they tend to be isolated and underfunded. If they are to have a major impact, they need to be supported to a much greater degree.

Economic Productivity

Although economic productivity has always been a goal of adult literacy education, as this nation's competitive position in the world economic order becomes increasingly threatened the goal of increased economic productivity has risen in prominence. The reasons for increased attention to economic productivity have been succinctly voiced by the United States Department of Labor's Commission on Workforce Quality and Labor Market Efficiency (1989): "America's ability to shape the course of the twenty-first century will depend largely on the productivity of the American workforce. Competitive advantage has replaced military might as the principal source of global influence. Our major trading partners have realized that their productivity will determine both their international power and standard of living. These countries have made substantial commitments to educate and train their workforces. America has, in many respects, failed to do the same" (p. 1).

Although nearly everyone seems to agree that increased productivity should be an important goal of adult literacy education, there are at least two policy issues which bear consideration. The first has to do with whether adult literacy policy favors the accumulation or redistribution of wealth; the second pertains to whether policy should favor economic growth or economic development.

Writing about Latin America, Sloan (1984) notes that political economies tend to favor one of two policy alternatives, accumulation or distribution. Accumulation policies are designed to generate national wealth. Reducing the capital gains tax is an example. The problem is, however, that when wealth is created in a market economy, it is generally created unequally to the extent that, without controls, the rich become richer and the poor become even poorer. Consequently, to promote social and economic equity, policies are needed that redistribute wealth from the most affluent to the poor. Progressive taxation is one method of redistribution; public subsidy of social programs that benefit the poor is another. Since adult literacy education clearly benefits the poor, the federal program has had important distribution effects. In fact, in order to receive federal funds under the Adult Education Act, states must submit state plans, and in their plans states are required to "describe how the particular educational needs of adult immigrants, the incarcerated, persons with handicaps, the chronically unemployed, the homeless, the disadvantaged and minorities will be addressed" (Adult Education Act, Sec 342, (c),(7)).

Yet in the hue and cry over productivity, and with the increasing emphasis on workplace literacy, this situation may be changing, and the federal program may be favoring accumulation more and more. This becomes evident when the question of who benefits from workplace literacy is considered. Business and industry benefit from the increased profits that productivity generates. Stockholders likewise benefit. Workers may benefit if their salaries increase. But who does not benefit? Welfare mothers, the unemployed, the neediest.

Policymakers involved in efforts to foster productivity through adult literacy education also need to consider whether the ultimate goal should be economic growth or economic development. Sloan (1984) notes that growth policies are directed to increases in output while economic development policy "involves the more efficient use of natural and human resources" (p. 23). While economic growth only considers productivity, economic development focuses on the broad based personal and social development of the poor as well.

Again these policy alternatives are played out in workplace literacy. Stein (1990) describes two approaches to workplace literacy, characterizing the first, which is equated with narrow economic growth, as the narrow technocratic view. This approach begins with a literacy audit designed to determine, "first, what literacy tasks are requisite to successful performance on the job and, second, whether individual workers who hold the position have the appropriate skills to fulfill those requirements" (p. 307). From the literacy audit, instructional objectives are derived which are specific to the performance of a particular job. Although individual productivity may be enhanced through this approach, the carry-over effects are at best minimal. While learners may learn to do their specific jobs better, they learn to do little else.

In contrast to the technocratic approach to workplace literacy, Stein describes an approach designed to capacitate workers broadly to "fully participate in all aspects of work life" (p. 312), an approach which focuses on economic development rather than narrow economic growth. In what might be termed the community development approach to workplace literacy, along with traditional literacy skills workers learn such things as decision making, how to work as a team, and how their work contributes to the business as a whole. As a result, not only are they able to do their individual jobs better, but they are able to contribute fully to the workplace community.

Learners' Own Goals

Society is willing to subsidize adult literacy education primarily because of its social benefits, benefits which accrue to all through decreased welfare payments and increased economic productivity. Learners, on the other hand, participate to accomplish their own goals which include such things as developing self-improvement, meeting family responsibilities, being more effective in their communities, and earning educational advancement (Beder & Valentine, 1987). Clearly, the ability of adult literacy to meet learners' goals is critical, as it is individual goal attainment which motivates participation. Indeed, society is able to reap its benefits from adult literacy education only if learners are able to reap theirs.

To some extent the desired outcomes for adult literacy education that are expressed in state and federal policy correspond well with learners' goals. As noted in the chapter on motivation, learners do want to advance in their jobs and to earn more; above all, they wish to earn high school credentials. As Valentine (1990) and Darkenwald and Valentine (1984) note, however, economic and occupational advancement may be less important to learners than to policy makers. Yet there are also significant discrepancies between the intended outcomes of policy makers and the actual outcomes of adult literacy education; the most striking discrepancies pertain to intrinsic outcomes, most particularly to enhanced self-concept.

An analysis of adult literacy impact studies leads to the conclusion that enhanced self-concept is the greatest and most universal outcome of adult literacy education. Yet policy statements, the Adult Education Act for example, treat enhanced self-concept as if it were a serendipitous side benefit or fail to mention it at all. As a state director of adult education notes (Iowa Literacy Studies Panel, 1989), "I find it politically difficult to sell the idea of saying the purpose of the program—when you are talking to a state or federal legislative body—has to do with self-improvement or self-esteem, even if we know that that's a really important by-product of the program or even the main thing people get out of it." Why? The answer may be that from a policy maker's perspective, enhanced self-concepts and other intrinsic outcomes are considered to be individual benefits which do not warrant public subsidy.

The issue is whether or not discrepancies between the desired outcomes of adult literacy education as voiced in public policy and those expressed by learners are a problem. To a certain extent the answer is "no," for at the local level the adult literacy education system seems to have been flexible enough to adapt to learners' goals (Iowa Literacy Studies Panel, 1989). At the same time, however, state and local adult literacy systems may be constrained from articulating their programs toward learners' goals by a need to show accountability to public policy.

WHO SHOULD BE SERVED?

The question of who should be served by adult literacy education is an eternal and vital issue. In addressing it, it is possible to identify two alternatives. On one hand, adult literacy education might concentrate on the neediest and hardest to reach; on the other, it might concentrate on the most motivated and most likely to participate. As important as the question may be, however, its resolution must take into account an important reality. Adult literacy education is a voluntary program; it can only serve those who choose to participate.

Who is most likely to participate? Research suggests that better educated, younger, and less socially alienated adults are the most likely candidates for adult literacy education and that this has resulted in what Mezirow, Darkenwald, and Knox (1975) term a "creaming" operation. Since program resource allocations are linked to enrollments, and since accountability is tied to successful completion rates, adult literacy programs tend to serve those who are easiest to attract and easiest to educate. This population, the one that is most likely to attend adult literacy education, has often been referred to as the demand population. Unfortunately, however, the demand population is but the tip of the proverbial iceberg. In fact, as Pugsley (1990) notes, "The national level of effort in tackling illiteracy reaches only 8 percent of the target population annually" (p. 1).

Some argue that focusing on the demand population makes good sense. In a free society, why induce adults to do things they choose not to do? Moreover, is it not better to concentrate scarce resources on those who are the most motivated to enroll in literacy education and therefore are the most likely to persist and benefit from it? There is a problem with this logic, however, and it is quite simple. To write off 92% of those eligible for adult literacy education represents an unacceptable social cost. Furthermore, as many emancipatory literacy educators would argue, demand for adult literacy education is socially constructed. Through the social reproduction process, some are induced *not* to desire additional schooling. If this is true, to concentrate service on the demand population would perpetuate social injustice.

Key to reaching the overwhelming majority of eligible adults who choose not to participate in adult literacy education is an understanding of the reasons for nonparticipation. As Beder (1989a) notes, there are at least four basic reasons: low perception of need, perceived effort, dislike for school, and situational barriers. Many adults do not perceive a need for adult literacy education because they have successfully adapted to low literacy, or despite not having completed high school, they have become literate on their own. Others perceive that adult literacy education will be too difficult, and this is quite understandable. Adult literacy education is a protracted enterprise fraught with many uncertainties. Some nonparticipants simply dislike school, although not necessarily learning. Still others are constrained by situational barriers, life circumstances that are beyond their control.

With the exception of situational barriers, the basic reasons for nonparticipation pertain to attitudes toward and beliefs about adult literacy education, and as Quigley (1989, 1990b) argues, these attitudes and beliefs are formed through previous experience with school. To the extent that nonparticipation is linked to attitudes and beliefs about school, nonparticipation is more than an adult education problem. It is a lifelong learning problem that must be addressed systemically at all levels rather than piecemeal.

Defining the target population for adult literacy education expediently as "adults who lack high school credentials," it is possible to divide the population into four groups based on an understanding of motivation and nonparticipation. The first is the demand population, those who want to participate and are not overly constrained. Although there are waiting lists for adult literacy education in some localities, by and large this group is being served. The second group consists of adults who wish to participate in adult literacy education, but are constrained by the life posed problems of adulthood. To secure their participation, the adult literacy delivery system needs to be expanded to include more supportive services. The provision of child care and literacy programs located in the workplace are positive steps in this direction.

The third group is comprised of adults who value literacy but, because of negative experiences with prior schooling, avoid anything to do with schools. It is not known exactly how many nonparticipants fall into this group, but according to Quigley (1989b) there are significant numbers. If these "resisters" are to be reached, new and better non-school models for adult literacy education must be developed. The last group consists of adults who have either adapted to low literacy and are functioning well, or who have acquired literacy skills through self-effort. In a static society, it would be difficult to conclude that this group needs adult literacy education, and indeed they are the least in need. Yet the literacy requirements of society are constantly being upgraded, and what constitutes successful adaptation to low literacy today, may not tomorrow.

HOW CAN LEARNERS BE ATTRACTED?

The Stigma

Given that the great majority of adults who are eligible for adult literacy education do not seek it, it is clear that attracting learners is a major problem. Why? As has been noted, perceived lack of need, perceived difficulty, dislike for school, and situational barriers are some of the reasons. Yet there may be a more fundamental reason, and it pertains to the stigma that is attached to low literacy in American society. Historically, illiteracy has been viewed as a national menace, an impending disaster, and a moral disgrace (Quigley, 1990a). By extension, the blame has been placed on low literates themselves. In a society which cherishes independence, low literates are perceived to be dependent. This is evident even in the language of the Adult Education Act. The stigma is reified by the popular media which has characterized illiterates as being incompetent, unproductive, and incapable of making informed decisions (Ehringhaus, 1990). Worse yet, as Fingeret (1985) notes, many adult literacy professionals embrace the logic of the stigma and, in doing so, perpetuate it.

It is quite possible that this stigma has two deleterious effects on participation. First, participation in adult literacy education amounts to public acknowledgement that one is illiterate, especially for those who are the least literate. Because of the stigma, many may prefer to hide their illiteracy. Second, as Freire (1970) notes, low literates may internalize the stigma and in doing so come to believe that they are simply incapable of succeeding in adult literacy education.

It follows that success in attracting the vast majority of low literates who do not participate in adult literacy education may require the de-stigmatization of illiteracy. This will not be easy; the stigma is deeply rooted. Yet through staff development perhaps we can begin to change the professional norms which support the stigma among the adult literacy community.

Aversion to School

If resistance theorists are correct, low literates' aversion to adult literacy education stems more from negative attitudes toward school than from an aversion to learning. Adult literacy education, the federal program in particular, is strongly associated with elementary and secondary schooling. Most adult literacy programs are administered by public schools, most are conducted in schools, and in many localities such as New Jersey teachers must be certified by the public school system. Clearly, those who would avoid school are likely to avoid adult literacy education as well.

In marketing terms, for many there is a negative demand for schooling and, as Kotler (1978) notes, when faced with negative demand the appropriate strategy is to identify the negative aspects of the product and change them. What do nonparticipant adults perceive the negative aspects of their public school experience to be? In a qualitative study of twenty low literates who were aware of adult literacy education but had chosen not to participate, Quigley (1989) provides the beginnings of an answer. A majority of Quigley's resisters reported that their public school teachers had been insensitive, uncaring, or patronizing. As students, they been perceived to be stupid and were subsequently "written off." Other resisters mentioned that they had joined peer groups that were in constant conflict with the school culture. Typed as discipline problems, their behavior was met with exercises of authority at which they rebelled. Still others believed that they had been the brunt of racial prejudice. As one of Quigley's subjects recounts, "What made me drop out of school was the problems I was havin' with the one teacher. I had got, let him gotten me so angry with things he was saying to me that I wasn't, I wasn't important, I was just another black person and black people wouldn't go far and especially black women and I felt so much anger and hate for that man until I lashed out at him . . . " (p. 7).

It seems that the aversion to school is to a great extent an aversion to the school culture, a culture which uses authority to control, a culture which supports some and abandons others. Ultimately, "school" takes on a highly negative symbolism for many of those who left it. Is it possible to disembed adult literacy education from school while still retaining the positive aspects of schooling? Experimentation and research are needed to provide the answers.

Lessons from Marketing

Marketing theory provides important guidance in developing strategies for attracting learners, and fundamental to marketing theory is the concept of exchange. In participating in adult literacy, learners exchange scarce resources such as their time for something they value more, literacy. The objective in securing participation, then, is to maximize the value of literacy education while reducing the cost of participation as much as possible. What is the value of literacy to learners? Clearly literacy has intrinsic value, such as self-improvement, being able to be more productive in the community and church, and in meeting family responsibilities. Likewise, there is extrinsic value to literacy, the value of obtaining high school certification, occupational advancement, and increased income (Beder, 1990b).

The adult literacy population is not homogeneous, however. Literacy has different value for different people. Given this reality, a differentiated marketing strategy may improve the ability of adult literacy education to attract learners. In a differentiated marketing strategy, the market is first segmented into subgroups according to the benefits each segment desires from literacy. Then, programs, promotional activities, and locations are designed to appeal specifically to each identified segment.

Younger adults, for example, represent one possible segment. Iowa research (Beder & Valentine, 1987) suggests that the need of young people to launch themselves in the adult world is a major motivation to attend adult literacy education. Research conducted in North Carolina (Fingeret, 1985) concurs. Socialization theory suggests that young adults need literacy to improve their status in the adult world and to better fulfill newly acquired adult roles such as spouse, parent, and worker. For the first time, many experience the stigma attached to low literacy, and negative experiences with prior schooling are fresh in their minds.

Promotional messages for young adults might stress the importance of literacy to parenting, occupational advancement, and personal independence while conveying the notion that adult literacy education is different from school. Instructional materials might deal with such topics as the logistics of finding a place to live, getting married, and choosing a job. Similarly, perhaps by co-sponsoring instruction with an organization oriented toward young adults, a location might be obtained that particularly appeals to youth.

HOW MIGHT ADULT LITERACY EDUCATION BEST BE PROVIDED?

The issue of how adult literacy education might best be provided pertains to the delivery system, the configuration of adult literacy education programs through which learners learn. The discussion here will focus on the adult literacy education workforce, fragmentation versus pluralism, and the deficit model of adult literacy education.

The Adult Literacy Education Workforce

Despite all the rhetoric attesting to the critical importance of adult literacy to the nation's wellbeing, 94% of the adult literacy teachers work part time, and 40% are unpaid volunteers. The number of full time teachers has declined 48% since 1980 (Pugsley, 1990). While organizations such as Literacy Volunteers of America and Laubach Literacy Action provide training to volunteers, the training is minimal given the complexity of the task.

Use of a part time and paraprofessional work force has many implications for the adult literacy education endeavor. On the positive side, this work force is inexpensive, and many low literates have been served who otherwise would not have been given funding levels. Yet there are negative ramifications as well. First, a part time work force has a low capacity for professional development. Part timers interact infrequently and the lack of a communication infrastructure precludes the sharing of information and new ideas. Since part time

teachers generally serve another primary occupation, if they do invest in their own professional development the investment is for
training in that primary occupation. Even when part timers and
volunteers are willing to invest in their professional development as
adult literacy education teachers, many simply lack the time. Second, with a part time workforce it is difficult to treat low literate
students holistically, to render to them the full range of services they
need. Generally speaking, part time teachers arrive, teach, and then
leave. Given this situation, they are unable to get to know learners
as real people who are endeavoring to solve a multiplicity of problems. Finally, many part time teachers simply lack the skills and
knowledge to do the job. Many have had no training at all as literacy
educators. While others have been trained as teachers in conjunction
with full time positions in elementary or secondary schools, few
receive training in the adult aspects of adult literacy education.
Consequently, there may be a tendency to employ child oriented
techniques inappropriately. As Fingeret (1984) notes, "The typical
instructional approach is very similar to that used with children,
beginning with diagnostic testing to identify subskills that require
remediation, providing instruction in those sub-skill areas, and testing again. Weber (1977) suggests that student progress may be far
below what learners could actually achieve if instructional programs
were able to depart from public school and child-oriented models
of instruction" (p. 31).

   Clearly, if adult literacy education is worth doing, it is worth
doing well. This requires a well trained, well paid, professional
workforce. To this end, the overreliance on part time teachers and
volunteers is anathema.

Fragmentation or Pluralism

Fragmentation

   When comparing the adult literacy education delivery system
to other educational systems such as the public schools or higher
education, many have concluded that the adult literacy system is
fragmented. At the national level, the Department of Education, the
Department of Labor, and the Department of Defense are all involved in adult literacy to one degree or another. At the state level
fragmentation is often compounded. In New Jersey, for example,
six different state departments administer adult literacy programs

(NJALL, 1990). In addition, private organizations such as Laubach Literacy Action and Literacy Volunteers of America conduct adult literacy education, as do private industry and privately funded community based organizations. As a recent report notes, the situation has been similar in California: "While there have been efforts to coordinate providers, it is difficult to claim that California's array of adult education programs constitutes a 'system,' particularly from the perspective of the consumer. There are tens of thousands of courses from which to choose and little consistency in the content of programs with the same or similar course titles. There is also a confusing array of providers, each with their own eligibility and funding requirements. In the area of adult literacy alone, there are 1,200 providers" (California State Department of Education, 1989, p. 11). In belief that fragmentation and duplication of service reduce efficiency, limit accountability, and confuse learners, many states such as California, Michigan, New York, New Jersey, and Massachusetts are developing strategic initiatives to coordinate and consolidate their adult literacy delivery systems.

Such efforts may be long overdue. Fragmentation does produce waste, and it does prevent a holistic approach to the problems that low literate adults experience. Yet efforts at coordination and consolidation raise some important issues as well. The first is accountability. Accountability to whom and according to what criteria? There are several possibilities. For reasons which have been mentioned several times in this volume, more and more the adult literacy program is being viewed as a human capital program designed to enhance the productivity of the nation's workforce. Should the public accountability of adult literacy education be linked directly to learners' economic productivity? If so, will that majority of the target population who are retired or nearing retirement continue to be underserved?

A second alternative is for accountability to be measured by learning gain. Indeed, the federal rules and regulations that resulted from the 1988 Amendments to the Adult Education Act require each state to evaluate its program by administering standardized testing to a representative sample of one third of its participants (United States Department of Education, 1989). Yet if learning gain becomes the standard for accountability, does it not become rational for local programs to concentrate service on the most able, those who are likely to show the greatest learning gain in the least amount of time?

If such a situation develops, what will happen to the least able and most in need? If either productivity or learning gain becomes the standard for accountability, will those programs which have community development and collective social action as their primary goal be entirely read out of the funding picture?

A third option for accountability argues that since adult literacy education is a voluntary activity, and since adults are responsible for their own actions, programs should be accountable to their learners' goals. By and large, such an argument has prevailed up until now. Yet as has been shown, learners' goals are often different from the goals espoused in public policy; many adult literacy education participants are more interested in the intrinsic benefits of literacy than in the extrinsic outcomes embodied in productivity or rapid learning gain. Will a move toward greater accountability make it inexpedient to articulate programming toward learners' goals? If so, adult literacy programs may find that attracting learners will become more and more difficult.

Along with a press toward greater accountability, many efforts to reduce fragmentation call for increased systematization and, at its extreme, systematization can lead to the kinds of standardization in curricula which characterize elementary, secondary, and higher education. In the public school sector, a national curriculum has evolved over time to the extent that what is taught in one school district differs little from what is taught in another. There are many sound reasons for such standardization in the public school sector, but do they apply to adult literacy education? While children are taught to read and write in a general sense within a school context that supports reading and writing in most learning activities, adults learn to read and write in order to function better in specific and varied contexts. Adults use, and thereby continue to develop, literacy skills to meet their own ends rather than the ends of school systems. Thus, although some systematization may be desirable to increase the efficiency and accountability of the adult literacy education program, any effort to parallel the standardization of elementary and secondary education may well eliminate the adultness from adult literacy education.

Pluralism

While some see fragmentation when they examine the adult literacy education delivery system, others define the same situation as pluralism. Adult literacy education as it now stands has evolved over time in response to regional differences and to the various literacy needs and desires of individuals and groups. True, as noted in the first chapter there are similarities among programs produced by commonly held professional norms and a strong linkage to the public school experience. Yet there are also many variations in the delivery system that have developed from the real need to adapt. As one participant in a policy oriented panel (Iowa Adult Literacy Studies Panel, 1989) noted, "So to what extent do we say that what has to happen is that all those levels have to be the same—what the federal government says, what the state says, what an individual institution says and what the individual student says—all have to be the same? I don't think that that's realistic. What I want is for a program to be organized in a way that within it there's the flexibility to be responsive to who the students are. And to make sure that the mission doesn't get defined in a way that keeps that from happening." The state director of adult education for a midwestern state echoes the point. "Policy should insure that programs can stay multidimensional so that they can meet the needs of as many students as possible . . . there's a lot of room in there [the federal program] for maneuvering."

In reality, although national objectives for adult literacy are written into federal policy, and although these policies are often embellished at the state level, at the local level adult literacy programs pursue individual and group needs as they find them. Although the result is defined as fragmentation by some, for others it is defined as pluralistic adaptation to different needs and conditions. It may be that although the delivery system would benefit from better coordination and strategic planning, its very strength and survival may lie in its pluralism. After all, adults are voluntary learners. Unless programs are flexible enough to meet individual needs, there will be no students to educate.

The Deficit Model Versus
the Participatory Literacy Model

The Deficit Model

The literature reviewed in this volume leads to the conclusion that the traditional model for adult literacy in the United States is a deficit model. Public adult literacy policy is based on the assumption that low literates lack the skills and knowledge needed for functioning in mainstream society. The professional norms of many adult literacy educators are founded on the belief that their students have lived lives of failure, that previous failure has resulted in generalized, negative self-concepts, and that, unless the deficits which have resulted in failure are fixed up, failure will repeat itself. This, as Fingeret (1985) notes, often leads teachers to take a condescending, patronizing stance toward their students. Indeed, the deficit model is reified by the teaching-learning technology of most traditional programs. The individual's deficits are diagnosed, typically through standardized testing, and a treatment is prescribed in expectation that the literacy "patient" will then become "well."

Yet the logic which supports the deficit model may be more myth than reality. First, although most low literates have failed to complete high school, many are quite successful. As Griffith (1990) reports, 40% of the Canadian adults with less than nine grades of formal education had incomes above the national average in 1980. Furthermore, although adult literacy education does seem to enhance self-concept, there is no conclusive evidence that the self-concepts of adult literacy students are lower than the self-concepts of the general population. There is certainly no convincing evidence to the effect that for adult literacy students negative self-concepts are a generalized personality trait produced by lives of failure. It may be that what is interpreted as low self-concept is simply the insecurity that most adults exhibit when undertaking something difficult and unknown. It may also be that while some adult literacy students do have negative self-concepts, the negativity is limited to the role of student. Furthermore, as Quigley's (1990b) research indicates, rather than considering leaving school to be a personal failure, for many low literates dropping out was a rational response to an intolerable situation.

If the deficit model does not rest on a firm foundation of fact, what perpetuates it? There are at least two possibilities. It may be that the deficit model provides the justificatory logic for the public subsidy of the adult literacy program. Society is weakened by *their* inability to function effectively in it. Thus, once *their* deficit is corrected, all tax payers benefit. It may also be, however, that the deficit model rests on the false logic of social stigma. The commonly held beliefs that support stigmatization have it that illiterates are unproductive and are undermining our ability to compete in the world economic order. Consequently, they cost hard working adults a great deal of money. Illiterates are believed to be lazy, stupid, or both. After all, in the United States everyone has an equal chance to become literate; if they did not become literate, something must be wrong with them. And finally, illiteracy is associated with crime, drug use, and family decay. By extension, then, illiteracy is also seen as immoral.

Stigmas are social constructions and as such fulfill social purposes. There are at least three possible reasons for perpetuating the stigma of illiteracy. First, the stigma may be no more than veiled racism. While it is no longer socially acceptable to publicly denigrate blacks, Hispanics, and welfare recipients, it is acceptable to denigrate them indirectly by denigrating illiterates. Second, in placing the blame for low productivity and a host of other social ills on illiterates, the blame is shifted from those who are truly responsible to those who are powerless to defend themselves. Finally, it may be that, as stigmatized, illiterates set a necessary bad example. We are exhorted to do well in school, to work hard, lest we end up like *them.*

The deficit model then feeds the very stigma which makes life success problematic for low literates. Additionally, in espousing it, the very group that should serve as the locus of advocacy for low literates unwittingly undermines them. Fortunately, there is an alternative to the deficit model.

The Participatory Literacy Model

Participatory literacy subsumes what was defined earlier as emancipatory literacy. As defined by such authors as Fingeret (1984, 1989) and Jurmo (1989), participatory literacy is based on a set of assumptions which differ markedly from those of the deficit model. For participatory literacy educators, although the culture of illiteracy is different from that of the dominant culture, it is not inferior. As Fingeret (1984) notes, "When illiterate adults are seen as participating in some alternative culture in which literacy is not as central [as it is] to the dominant culture, the causes of illiteracy are culturally related, but not necessarily because the alternative culture is bad. This view respects the dignity and power of individuals through whose eyes the culture is viewed" (p. 14). When "deficits" are defined as differences, and when differences are respected, the stigma—and all that goes with it—begins to evaporate.

Participatory literacy is collaborative. Rather than merely receiving instruction, learners "help to define, create, and maintain the program" (Fingeret, 1989, p. 5). It is also learner centered. Learners are assisted in clarifying their own goals. Teachers then serve as facilitators, helping learners to attain their goals. Power is not vested in literacy professionals. Rather, students and professionals share the power.

It is possible to discern two thought traditions which support a participatory model. The first is the liberal-progressive tradition championed by writers such as Lindeman (1926) and Knowles (1970, 1980). In this tradition, adult learners are viewed as being responsible for their own actions, as being motivated by a desire to solve specific, life posed problems, and as bringing a wealth of prior experience to teaching-learning transactions. It follows that the mission of adult education, and of adult literacy education in specific, is to facilitate learners' own goal attainment rather than to convey the knowledge deemed to be appropriate by experts.

The second tradition, which is often associated with the work of Paulo Freire, considers illiteracy to be a social construction which supports the hegemony of the dominant social classes. This is the tradition of emancipatory literacy and, as has been noted many times in this volume, the objective is to create critical awareness of the social forces which create illiteracy so that they can be changed through collective social action.

Emancipatory literacy educators often note what seems to be a paradox. Although according to their view adult literacy education should be directed toward social change, when given the choice learners seem to prefer traditional literacy models designed to provide secondary school certification as rapidly and efficiently as possible. Although social change is important—perhaps even vital—given the demand for secondary school certification, it is certainly important to provide this certification. Yet there is no sound reason why the traditional, certification oriented model for adult literacy has to maintain a deficit orientation. Indeed, the participatory model is just as pertinent to meeting learners' certification goals as the deficit model is.

CONCLUSION

There are several themes which have been woven consistently throughout this volume, sometimes overtly, sometimes implicitly.

The first is that, however defined, adult literacy education is vitally important—important for national productivity, important for social justice, and important to the lives of those who, by fate, are unable to decode meaning stored in symbolic form. The second is that although low literates lack an important skill, they are not inferior as people. Indeed, to stigmatize them as being inferior makes it all the more difficult to collaborate with them on solving the problem. Finally, although low literacy poses problems for individuals, illiteracy itself is socially constructed and is unlikely to disappear unless the social mechanisms which support it are changed.

CHAPTER 7

Recommendations

In this concluding chapter I offer general recommendations for practice and research. The intent is not to prescribe. Rather, the intent is to stimulate dialogue and discussion in anticipation that the deliberations that may follow may lead to positive reform. It is important to note here that in recommending one must necessarily advocate one course of action over alternatives, and this precludes a nonjudgmental stance. My recommendations, therefore, reflect judgments which are influenced by my own point of view as well as by the research and theory discussed in previous chapters.

RECOMMENDATIONS FOR PRACTICE

Recommendation One

The deficit orientation which pervades the federal adult literacy program must be changed.

After an extensive review of the adult literacy education literature, Fingeret (1984) concluded, "Literacy educators have been influenced deeply by the perspective emerging from the War on Poverty in the 1960s, which portrayed individuals as embedded in a culture of poverty. . . . The culture-of-poverty approach has been labeled a deficit perspective, in which middle class culture is established as the norm and other cultures are judged against its characteristics. The deficit perspective has been criticized extensively, but its prevalence in the literature is striking. Many authors cite the fact that illiterate adults bring a wealth of experience and a fully developed language system to the teaching-learning interaction; however, fear of failure, low self-esteem and self-confidence, resistance to change and lack of future orientation, inarticulateness, fatalism, inability to cope or to think abstractly, and apathy of illiterate adults are mentioned much more often. The disadvantaged are portrayed as poor financial planners, parents, housekeepers, friends and spouses" (p. 13).

The deficit perspective is reflected in the language of the Adult Education Act which characterizes low literate adults as being dependent and unable to function effectively. It pervades the professional norms of adult literacy professionals (Fingeret, 1984, 1985) and it guides teaching methodologies which begin with the diagnosis of deficits and then prescribe instruction to correct them. Learners are conceived to be lacking; teachers are experts at mending.

It is possible to identify two separate components of the deficit perspective. The first pertains to literacy skill deficit defined as the discrepancy between a learner's reading, writing and mathematical skills and the desired level of skill performance. Understanding the magnitude and nature of the deficit enables teachers to treat it to the learner's benefit. Although there are alternatives to skill oriented approaches to teaching literacy education, the skill oriented approach is systematic, adapts well to individualized instruction, and is generally effective.

The second component of the deficit perspective focuses on social deficit, and it contains all the elements that Fingeret aptly portrays. Middle class society is viewed as being healthy, desirable, and the object of low literates' aspirations, while the lower class subculture is deemed to be dysfunctional, inferior, and morally impoverished. Unlike literacy skill deficit, the social deficit perspective is far from innocuous; indeed, it may cause great damage. This is so for at least two reasons.

First, the social deficit perspective derives from, feeds, and perpetuates the stigma which society attaches to illiteracy. Illiterates are denigrated and discriminated against. As Goffman (1974) notes, in fear of such social sanctions the stigmatized often respond by "covering," by hiding the stigmatizing condition. Since participation in adult literacy education requires low literates to publicly disclose their illiteracy—to "blow their cover" so to speak—many may feel it is simply safer to stay away.

Second, the social deficit perspective promotes an instructional milieu where teachers are socially superior to learners, where teachers are guides and learners are guided, where the knowledge teachers bring to the teaching-learning situation is valued and learners' knowledge is not valued, and where learning needs are determined by experts rather than by learners themselves. While this instructional milieu may be appropriate for children in a public school context, it runs counter to sound adult education practice as advocated by theorists from Lindeman (1926) to Knowles (1970, 1980), theorists who feel that adults should be respected as being autonomous human beings capable of making their own choices, that the knowledge which adults bring to the teaching-learning situation should be valued and should serve as an important resource for learning, that instruction should be designed to meet needs as expressed by learners, and that adult learners should participate in designing their own educational programs.

A pointed critique of the deficit perspective is not meant to be an indictment of adult literacy teachers who for the most part mean well, work hard, and deeply care for their students. Rather, it is meant to point out that the deficit perspective demeans the subculture from which adult literacy students come. It hinders teachers from comprehending the meanings their students ascribe to the world, and it prohibits teachers from gearing instruction to their students' own experience. If the deficit model is to be eliminated, adult literacy education professionals need to achieve a much better understanding of their students' culture of orientation. They must also be helped to critically assess a child oriented conception of education based on prior experience with elementary and secondary education. This is clearly a role for staff development and graduate education and should be a major priority.

Recommendation Two

In order to serve a greater proportion of the adult literacy target population, recruitment and instruction should be tailored to specific client group needs, wants, and motivations.

As has been shown in the chapters of this volume dealing with participation and nonparticipation, the adult literacy target population is far from homogeneous. Rather, it is composed of many subgroups which have different needs and are motivated to attend for different reasons. A wealth of marketing theory (Beder, 1980, 1986; Kotler, 1975) suggests that, if recruitment messages and media were "differentiated" to appeal to specific group needs and motivations, recruitment would be enhanced. Likewise, if instruction were focused on specific group needs and motivations, greater numbers would participate and persist.

From a practical perspective, however, how to differentiate the delivery system is a more difficult problem than whether to differentiate it. In fact, the delivery system has always been differentiated to some degree. The Adult Education Act, for example, targets the incarcerated, the handicapped, and the homeless as priority groups. Yet in the case of the Adult Education Act, and in federal policy in general, differentiations have been made according to political priorities which derive from social needs. While this may be desirable, it is individual needs and motivations that induce voluntary learners to participate. Thus, if participation is to be increased, differentiation must also focus on configurations of individual needs and motivations as well as on social priorities.

In Chapter Six the target population was divided into four groups which may serve as a framework for differentiation. The first group, defined as the demand population, is comprised of those who are motivated to participate and are not overly constrained from doing so. This is the group the federal program currently serves. Iowa research (Beder & Valentine, 1987,1990) suggests that the demand population is motivated by a desire for educational advancement, self-improvement, literacy development, better community and church involvement, economic gain, meeting family responsibilities, diversion, job advancement, and launching into a new life, and is motivated by a desire to please others as well. These multifaceted motivations might serve as the basis for further differentiation of the demand population.

The second group consists of those who wish to participate in adult literacy education, but are constrained by life imposed problems or by lack of access to programs. The provision of more programming with different scheduling and location options is the key to reaching this group, and an increase in resources will undoubtedly be required if we are to do so.

The third group is comprised of adults who value literacy, but avoid school because of negative experiences with prior schooling. For the most part, we are not reaching this group with current programming. If we are to reach them, adult literacy education must disassociate itself from the symbolic elements of schools which are distasteful. Although community based adult literacy education is a step in the right direction, it may well be that we must develop entirely new educational models if we are to substantially reach this group. This should be a major priority for future research and development.

The fourth group consists of adults who have learned to compensate for their low literacy and are functioning well or have acquired literacy through self-learning. We know little about this group and they are the least in need of adult literacy education. The level of literacy required by society is constantly increasing, however, and those who function well today may find it difficult to function in the future.

Recommendation Three

Adult literacy policy and practice must recognize that literacy is a lifelong learning problem and that a coordinated lifelong learning strategy is needed to solve it.

Illiteracy is a cultural phenomenon; the path to adult illiteracy begins at birth for the inner city and rural poor, blacks, Hispanics, and other groups born into social disadvantage. For groups such as these there is a discontinuity between their cultures of orientation and the social institutions of the dominant society. For them the values, social organization, and role relationships of the public schools are alien and alienating. In Bordieu and Passerson's (1977) terms, they lack the cultural capital to compete. Consequently, large percentages of the disadvantaged leave school. Some later return to adult literacy education; most do not.

It follows that adult illiteracy is more than an adult education problem. It is a lifelong learning problem, and if it is to be substantially reduced a coordinated lifelong learning strategy is needed that touches all levels of our educational system. Such a strategy should have two thrusts. First, the fragmentation of effort which exists at all levels must be reduced. At the federal level the Departments of Education, Labor, Defense, and Agriculture all deal with literacy to some extent and in some form, yet coordination among them is minimal. Likewise, while public school, higher, and adult education all acknowledge that adult low literacy is a problem, their efforts to deal with it are for the most part separate. Discussing the political aspects of the fragmentation issue, Chisman (1990) notes, "At the

federal, state and local levels of government, responsibility is dis-
persed among education, job-training, and welfare agencies. . . .
Realistically, close collaboration is unlikely under this governance
structure. For example, it is hard to imagine welfare officials making changes necessary to fully integrate literacy into their service
systems, just as it is hard to imagine most educators fully understanding or accepting the complexities and constraints of the welfare
system" (p. 261).

It is true that the disparate agencies that provide literacy education do often cooperate. As mentioned in the first chapter, for
example, adult literacy education is greatly influenced by its association with the public schools, and the federal program administered by the Department of Education often provides instruction to
private industry councils administered through the Department of
Labor.

Yet, as beneficial as such cooperation may be, it tends to be
sporadic and ad hoc. Coordinated strategic planning and initiatives
have been lacking. A strategic plan must first recognize that since
illiteracy is a lifelong learning problem that begins in preschool
experience and continues throughout adulthood, all levels of the
educational system must be involved in the solution. Then we must
achieve consensus about the causes of illiteracy. This may necessitate
a vastly expanded research effort, particularly in the area of policy
research. Finally, coordinated and integrated interventions must be
planned that fall under the authority of a single agency, perhaps, as
Chisman (1990) advocates, a newly constituted Department of Human Services established through the merger of the Departments of
Education and Labor.

A second thrust of a lifelong literacy approach should focus
directly on prevention. Family literacy programs which impact on
both adults and their children are a promising development in this
regard. Noting that until recently adult literacy education has focused solely on the low literate adult, Fingeret (1990) writes, "In
the past, this is where most adult literacy programs would stop.
Now, however, there is pressure to intervene in the 'cycle' of illiteracy; and so this mother is viewed as part of a family network that
includes her children, her spouse, and others" (p. 34).

Many school based efforts at preventing illiteracy are oriented
toward correcting individual deficits, and these efforts are impor-

tant. Yet substantial success at preventing illiteracy will require systematic intervention in the social systems that create and maintain it.

Recommendation Four

The federal adult literacy education program should be held accountable for the broad personal and social development of its clients rather than to narrow human capital outcomes.

As has been pointed out throughout this volume there is a some disparity between the stated goals of the federal adult literacy program and the individual goals of its clients. To a certain extent this is understandable since the federal program has been designed to meet social goals while individuals participate to attain their own goals. The social goals of the federal program are significantly influenced by human capital arguments. It is believed that this nation's economic productivity is threatened by the low literacy of its workforce. When investments in adult literacy education increase productivity, the benefits that result accrue to all taxpayers. Although the human capital justification for public subsidy of adult literacy education has always been important, as the nation's productivity becomes a more and more critical issue human capital becomes more and more prominent. This is evident in a number of recent and influential policy analyses, most notable being the Hudson Institute's *Workforce 2000* (Johnson & Packer, 1987) and the Southport Institute's *Jump Start* report (Chisman, 1989). It is also evident in an increasing federal emphasis on workplace literacy.

When the reasons why adults participate in literacy education are considered, however, it becomes clear that most are seeking to improve themselves in many ways that go well beyond human capital. While participants do want to further their educations and to secure better employment, they are also motivated by the desire for general self-improvement and by the desire to be more effective in their social roles (Beder & Valentine, 1987, 1990). While the impact studies reviewed in Chapter Five do show human capital gains, they also suggest that improved self-concept is the greatest impact of the federal program.

Is the discrepancy between stated policy and practice a problem? At present probably not. In fact the notoriety surrounding the human capital crisis has promoted an increase in adult literacy education resources while in practice adult literacy education programs have not been prevented from meeting learners' needs and goals as they find them. Yet along with increased notoriety have come increased calls for accountability. As Chisman (1990) writes, "Today, literacy service in America is almost entirely input-driven. Resources are allocated on the basis of the number of learners served, the numbers of hours of service, the cost of materials, or other input measures, and the success of programs evaluated, if at all, in terms of whether these input measures have been met. This accountant's mentality pays little or no attention to what should be the major basis for allocating resources or measuring success: how much learners achieve, and in particular, whether their achievements make a difference in their employment prospects or in their everyday lives. . . . This must change. The nation is unlikely to invest large new resources in a system that is not designed to reward success and penalize failure" (p. 257).

No one would argue that adult literacy education should not be held accountable, but to whom and to what? Herein lies a major problem. Society can reap its benefits only if voluntary learners reap theirs. Thus, if programs were held accountable to a narrow range of human capital goals, programs would find it very difficult to focus instruction on the goals of those learners who care little for human capital concerns. Participation would suffer; the proverbial baby would be thrown out with the proverbial bath. When accountability is tightened, the discrepancy between human capital concerns and learner's goals becomes very much of an issue.

There are several ways to solve the problem. First, it might be officially recognized that the federal program must be accountable to the attainment of learners' goals regardless of whether or not they focus on human capital concerns. This would formally recognize that adult literacy education is much more than an investment in human capital. This is the honest approach, the one advocated here. Yet it may also be the most difficult approach to achieve politically. Alternatively, it might be acknowledged that criteria for accountability should vary from program to program depending on programmatic context and the kind of learners served. For example, adult literacy education programs that focus on social change might be permitted to evaluate themselves on criteria which differ markedly from those of workplace literacy programs. Such an accountability system would permit adult literacy programs to articulate toward specific learner and community needs, but would it satisfy those who are clamoring for greater accountability? Probably not.

The third alternative is simply to leave things as they are, to recognize that the adult literacy education system must be driven by social needs at the top and by individual needs at the bottom. This path requires us to tolerate contradiction. Yet given its conceptual and programmatic complexity, adult literacy education tolerates many contradictions.

Recommendation Five

The delivery system for adult literacy education should retain its flexible, adaptive, pluralistic orientation.

Although the federal adult literacy program can be criticized on several counts, clearly it has been highly successful in adapting to local conditions and needs. In areas of low target population density, for example, a one room schoolhouse model of instruction has emerged, while, where larger concentrations of low literate adults permit, comprehensive adult learning centers have been established. Since the skill levels of adult literacy students vary considerably, and because adults come and go as their lives permit, a highly individualized form of instruction has developed in most locales. In programs that face chronic resource scarcity, volunteers have been used extensively as instructors and aides. In Iowa the federal program is administered through community colleges, in Wisconsin through vocational schools, and in many other states through public schools. Unions, businesses, and community based organizations all receive funds through the Adult Education Act. Some local programs employ a competency based approach to instruction; others use traditional methods, and still others employ an emancipatory education approach.

Adult literacy education is a tapestry of diversity. Yet with the diversity that derives from the need to adapt comes a marked lack of standardization. For example, while attention to reading, writing, and mathematics is common to all programs, there are considerable differences in the amount of learning gain expected. Indeed, in fear that a rigorous attention to learning gain will drive students away, many programs adopt a posture of minimum failure and in doing so maximize attendance over gain per hour of instruction (Mezirow, Darkenwald, & Knox, 1975). Likewise, for some programs reading, writing, and mathematics are but the means to some other end such as functional literacy or community activism.

Diversity and its consequence—a low degree of standardization—are an asset and a necessary response to the adultness of adult literacy education. Unlike children, adults choose their own educational goals—goals which vary considerably. Unlike children, adults' abilities to attend literacy education are contingent on resolving life posed problems that often interrupt their education and make learning difficult. Unlike the public schools, adult literacy education programs find it difficult to group their students into units such as grades or tracks.

However, diversity poses problems in respect to accountability and coordination that have caused some to call for a much greater degree of standardization. It is argued that accountability is necessary to protect the public's interest in the federal program, to inspire public confidence, and to protect adult learners from malfeasance. However, accountability generally requires that standardized assessment criteria be applied to evaluation, and this promotes standardization at the expense of diversity. Consider the consequence of mandating a standard of accountability through a tested learning gain in reading, writing, and mathematics. Would it be tempting for some programs to ignore the slowest and least able students, the ones who are likely to show the least learning gain? Would programs which view literacy to be a means to another end be forced to abandon their goals in favor of rigorous attention to test performance? Quite possibly. Standardized criteria for accountability will require standardized program goals and methods of operating. In the long run, adult literacy education might lose its very vitality.

As noted in Chapter Six, when some contemplate the diversity of adult literacy education they conclude that the delivery system is fragmented and in need of major consolidation. It is claimed that fragmentation causes waste, confuses learners, and prevents a holistic approach to the multifaceted problems the disadvantaged experience. To a great extent these claims have merit. Fragmentation should be reduced, but not at the expense of diversity and the ability to adapt. At issue, perhaps, is the difference between consolidation and coordination.

Consolidation entails a reduction in the number of adult literacy providers, tight goal consensus, and accountability to a common authority which has the power to sanction noncompliance. As defined here, consolidation is anathema to a pluralistic, flexible delivery system. Coordination, on the other hand, focuses on more fully integrating the parts of the delivery system through better communication and cooperation. Learners benefit and diversity is maintained.

Notable efforts at coordination in California and New York are designed to provide holistic service to adult learners. In California's proposed "EduCard" system (California State Department of Education, 1989), potential learners would access adult education through a community adult education service center. At the center, clients would present their EduCards (Adult Education Access Card) to gain accesses to their educational records and program eligibility status stored in an integrated adult education data system. The data system would provide information on the learner's skill attainment and educational needs according to standard performance measures used by all participating programs. Additional assessment could be requested and the results would be entered into the data system. After assessment, potential learners would be presented with an impartial description of programs that might meet their needs; a program would be selected, and learners would be enrolled electronically. Programs would be financed through a common pool of funds "billed" through the EduCard for the educational service. The results of students' performance in the program would be fed back into the students' record in the data system.

New York's ACCESS Centers (NJALL, 1990) are a collaborative venture between the State Departments of Education, Social Services, and Labor. A full range of services is provided at each ACCESS site including learning assessment, literacy education, occupational training, counseling, job development and placement. Thus rather than having to seek service from a wide array of agencies to solve their problems, students can meet all their service needs in one place.

To summarize, far from representing chaos, the pluralism and diversity of the federal adult literacy program has been a functional response to the need to adapt. While accountability and the elimination of fragmentation are important goals, efforts to attain them will be counterproductive if in the long run they rob the program of its flexibility.

Recommendation Six

While adult literacy programs designed to promote social and economic opportunity should be maintained, a substantial reduction in adult illiteracy will require an expansion of programming designed to change the social conditions which cause illiteracy.

While the acquisition of reading, writing, and mathematical skills may be positive ends in their own right, it is clear that for both policy makers and learners literacy is primarily considered to be the means to an end. For policy makers the ultimate outcome for adult literacy is a more equal and productive social order. For learners the desired outcome is simply a better life, however conceived. Yet while there is general consensus on the ultimate goals of adult literacy education, there is much less agreement on how to achieve them.

As has been suggested several times in this volume, there are two contrasting positions regarding the social role of adult literacy education. The first is the economic opportunity position; the second is the social change position. The economic opportunity argument undergirds the federal adult literacy program. Proponents argue that by providing programs which enable the disadvantaged to acquire skills required for middle class functioning, clients can and will rise in the social order. The focus is generally on individual skill acquisition. Some programs focus primarily on reading, writing, and mathematical skills; others also focus on the functional competencies that are presumably needed for social and economic life success. A recent list of competencies published by CASAS (1990), for example, includes over 230 life skills competencies.

As the impact studies cited in Chapter Five attest, the federal adult education program does promote social and economic opportunity. Traditional adult literacy programs do enable learners to secure better jobs, increase their incomes, and continue their educations. However, the federal adult literacy program serves only those upwardly mobile adults who are motivated to participate in it, currently estimated by the government to be about 8% of the target population. Although the federal adult literacy program certainly provides important benefits and should be strengthened and maintained, given participation rates it is clear that it alone cannot solve the adult illiteracy problem. Why?

It is quite possible that the great majority of those who elect not to participate in traditional programs are embedded in a "subculture of illiteracy" associated with social class. This subculture fails to perceive a need for literacy, perceives literacy acquisition to be too arduous, and avoids school which is simply disliked. The subculture of illiteracy is a structural phenomenon maintained by social forces. It thrives in the inner city and in pockets of rural poverty. Many theorists believe that this subculture is constantly being reproduced through our social institutions, most notably the schools, to insure an adequate supply of labor at the bottom tier. Society needs an under class to do the kinds of work only an under class does.

If illiteracy is socially constructed, it follows that it can only be eliminated if the social forces which produce it are modified. This logic is the basis for the second position on the social role of adult literacy education, the social change position. Although those who hold this view go by many labels, including emancipatory educator, popular educator, and transformative educator, their prescriptions for adult literacy education are similar. They believe that since it is in the interest of the dominant society to maintain a culture of illiteracy, the social forces that produce illiteracy can only be changed by the collective action of low literates themselves. Yet to change the social forces that maintain illiteracy, low literates must first become critically aware of them. As Freire and Macedo (1987) note, facilitating this critical awareness becomes the primary goal for adult literacy education. While reading, writing, and mathematical skills are considered to be important, their value lies in their ability to aid critical reflection and social action rather than in their ability to promote individual social and economic mobility.

The notion that a substantial reduction of illiteracy will require considerable social change including the reallocation of educational, power, and monetary resources to the disadvantaged is threatening to many. Likewise, the collective empowerment of the disadvantaged to bring about such changes will undoubtedly create social dislocation. Yet if we are truly serious about solving the adult illiteracy problem, there may be no other alternative.

RECOMMENDATIONS FOR RESEARCH

Recommendation One

The effects of adult literacy education should to be determined through controlled, longitudinal impact studies.

All major impact studies of adult literacy education conducted to date have suffered from two critical flaws, lack of experimental control and a failure to measure long term impact. Because of the lack of experimental controls, after spending millions of dollars on adult literacy education over the past twenty years we still do not know for sure whether the federal program produces its desired outcomes. For example, at least two major impact studies (Kent, 1973; Darkenwald & Valentine, 1984) found increases in income for adult literacy education students. However, without controls it is impossible to know whether adult literacy education *caused* the increase or whether the increases were due to upturns in the economy or to the general ability and motivation of the adult literacy education participants.

To achieve experimental control is logistically difficult. True experimental research designs which feature random assignment to treatment and control groups on a large scale are expensive and disruptive to programs. Yet it may be quite possible to design quasi experimental impact studies which compare completers of adult literacy education to carefully selected groups of nonparticipants and which control for possible sources of bias through regression analysis or other statistical and design procedures. The results of this extra care would be well worth the effort expended.

It is also important to measure the long term impact of adult literacy education through longitudinal studies, for it is quite possible that impact is cumulative. Adult literacy education may have an enabling effect. It may, for example, enable completers to achieve better incomes which are then invested in such things as further education, higher education for their children, retirement, and health care. While the short term effects of adult literacy education may be modest, the long term effects compounded over a life time may be enormous.

The most difficult problem with longitudinal studies is finding adequate numbers of adult literacy education students after a considerable amount of time has elapsed. A GED follow up study now under way in Iowa (Hartwig, 1990), however, demonstrates that to do so is not impossible. Iowa GED completion records going back 10 years are coded with students' social security numbers. Current driver's license data is also coded by social security number. By matching the social security numbers of students who passed the GED 10 years ago with social security numbers on current drivers' licenses, current addresses are being obtained. Through this procedure, it is estimated that over 80% of the 1980 GED completers will be located in 1990.

Recommendation Two

The relationship between nonparticipation in adult literacy education and adults' previous school experience needs to be better understood.

Recent work by Quigley (1989,1990b) suggests that there is a strong connection between adults' elementary and secondary school experience and a reluctance to participate in adult literacy education. The cultures from which the poor and disadvantaged come often conflict with the culture of the schools; students resist school, drop out, and carry their negative perceptions of school into adulthood. Although Quigley's work breaks important ground, it is just a beginning. We need to know more. We need to know just how important prior experience with schooling is in order to develop a better understanding of nonparticipation. We need to identify those aspects of schooling which are particularly distasteful to nonparticipants, and we need to know more about the mechanisms that produce the kinds of conflict in schools that eventually sour adults' attitudes toward the institution. If such research establishes a strong connection between culture, prior schooling, and nonparticipation, and if we can understand the basis of negative attitudes toward school, we will better understand how to prevent illiteracy and how to develop adult literacy education models that are successful in reaching chronic nonparticipants.

At this point we probably do not know enough about the connection between prior schooling and nonparticipation to engage in theory based hypothesis testing. Thus qualitative research will most likely net the most valuable results. Two types of studies would be valuable. The first would approach the problem at the public school level and would focus on school culture through ethnographic analysis similar to that of Willis (1978) as discussed in Chapter Four. The second would focus on adult nonparticipants using in depth interviews and a grounded theory methodology. While valuable in their own right, these studies would be an important step in recognizing an important reality—the reality that illiteracy is a lifelong learning problem and must be treated as such in research as well as in practice.

Recommendation Three

We need to better understand why the great majority of adults who are eligible for adult literacy education programs do not participate.

It is easy to conclude that the most critical problem facing adult literacy education is its inability to reach the great majority of those who are eligible for it. Clearly if we are to solve this problem we need to achieve a much better understanding of nonparticipation. To do so we need to address the causes of nonparticipation, and we need to refine our understanding of participation and nonparticipation.

In respect to causes, as Chapter Four suggests, there has been some promising recent work. Studies by Hayes (1987, 1988), Beder (1989a), and Quigley (1989, 1990b) suggest that nonparticipation is not simply a function of insurmountable structural barriers. Rather, nonparticipation is caused by deep-seated attitudes toward adult literacy education produced through social interaction. These studies, however, are but a beginning. Whether their findings generalize well beyond their study populations is not known and will not be known until there are replications and large scale analyses. Likewise, there are many issues in regard to nonparticipation that have not even been addressed through research. For example, it has always been assumed that poor self-concept and low self-esteem have contributed to nonparticipation. Indeed, these assumptions are fundamental to the deficit perspective. Yet the literature reviewed for this volume failed to uncover a single credible study which investigated the relationship between nonparticipation, self-esteem, or self-concept.

We need to understand the impact of culture and life history on nonparticipation. Are there important differences, for example, between older nonparticipants who lack high school simply because high school was not available to them and those younger nonparticipants who left school because they chose to or were forced out? How many of those who are labeled nonparticipants have learned to read and write well through self-education? If adults do become literate through self-education, how do they? The answer might form the foundation of entirely new models of adult literacy education.

There are two reasons, perhaps, why nonparticipation has not been adequately studied. First, it is very expensive to develop representative samples of nonparticipants. Yet given the magnitude of the nonparticipation problem and the social costs it represents, the money would be well spent. Second, it is questionable whether participation and nonparticipation have been adequately conceived. Federal data collection, for example, assumes that participation is an either-or proposition. In a given year, a given member of the target population is considered to be either a participant or a nonparticipant, and this results in the often cited participation figure of 8%. Yet there is anecdotal evidence which suggests that in reality participation is often serial. Learners enroll, "stop out," begin anew, again stop out, and continue thus until they either meet their goals or finally give up. If serial participation is common, then the either-or method of conceiving it is misleading and may seriously inflate the nonparticipation rate. To develop an accurate conception of nonparticipation, research is needed on *how* adults participate as well as on why they do not.

Recommendation Four

We need to refine our understanding of what motivates adults to participate in adult literacy education.

Essentially there are two ways to secure participation in adult literacy education. We can stimulate voluntary attendance by providing education geared to adults' motivations for learning, or we can induce attendance by threatening nonparticipants with sanctions. With the advent of the JOBS (Job Opportunities and Basic Skills) program funded under the Family Support Act there seems to be a trend towards induced participation. However, in a free society inducing adults to do something they would choose not to do raises valid and important ethical issues. Clearly, it is more desirable to secure voluntary attendance than it is to require it.

To secure voluntary participation it is necessary to gear instruction and recruitment to learners' motivations for learning and to be able to do this it is first necessary to know what learners' motivations are. Research reported in Chapter Three suggests that motivation is multifaceted, that while some learners are motivated to obtain extrinsic benefits such as increased incomes or better jobs, others are more motivated by intrinsic factors such as general self-improvement or the desire for more effective social participation. Most learners are motivated by multiple factors. For example, Iowa research (Beder & Valentine, 1987) designed to segment the participant population according to motivational orientations identified a predominantly female group who tended to be married and have children in the home. This group was most motivated by a desire to better meet family responsibilities and by a desire for educational advancement and, compared to other groups identified by the research, was relatively less motivated by the desire for literacy development, the desire to read, write, and compute, or by the desire for diversion.

Although the work on motivation needs to be expanded considerably, researchers should be aware of an important problem. As Usher and Bryant (1989) note, most academic research is designed to yield generalized propositions which confirm, disconfirm, and build theory. Yet if we are to facilitate voluntary attendance by targeting instruction on learners' motivations, we need to understand what motivates learners within specific practice contexts. Although knowledge of general motivation theory may be of some guidance to programmers, of much greater importance is knowledge of what motivates learners in Harlem or Cedar Rapids or a local prison or any other place where practice is being conducted. Thus, not only should theory based research on motivation be expanded, but applied, context specific research must be expanded also.

CONCLUSION

It is difficult to summarize a book in a concluding chapter, and it is just as difficult to summarize a concluding chapter in a paragraph. Nevertheless it is possible to derive the following principles from the 10 preceding recommendations, principles which may aptly serve as the last word to this volume.

1. It is ultimately more useful to conceive adult illiteracy as being a social construction maintained by social forces than it is to view illiteracy as being a collection of individual deficits spawned by personal failure. Let us stop blaming the victims and place the responsibility for illiteracy where it deserves to be—with all of us.

2. That the great majority of those who are eligible for the federal adult literacy program do not participate is a very serious problem. To solve it we need to differentiate service to meet the multiplicity of individual needs; we need to understand the non-participation problem much better, and we need to develop new models of adult literacy education which will appeal to nonparticipants.

3. The adult literacy program has been highly successful in adapting to local needs and conditions. While lack of standardization has resulted in calls for consolidation and common standards of accountability, policies that limit the adaptive, pluralistic orientation of the adult literacy education are likely to destroy its very adultness and vitality.

4. While human capital outcomes provide a social justification for the federal adult literacy education program, learners participate for a wide array of reasons which include, but are not limited to, human capital concerns. Adult literacy education must focus on meeting learners' goals, for as long as participation is voluntary society can reap its benefits only if learners are able to reap their own.

REFERENCES

Adult Performance Level Project. (1975). *Adult functional competency: A summary.* Austin, TX: University of Texas at Austin,
Division of Extension.

Anderson, R., & Darkenwald, G. (1979). *Participation and persistence in American adult education.* New York: College Entrance
Examination Board.

Aslanian, C. B., & Brickell, H. M. (1980). *Americans in transition:
Life changes as reasons for adult learning.* New York: College
Entrance Examination Board.

Association for Community Based Education. (1986a). *Adult literacy: A study of community based literacy programs* (Vol. 1,
Study Findings and Recommendations). Washington, DC: Association for Community Based Education.

Association for Community Based Education. (1986b). *Adult lit-
eracy: A study of community based programs* (Vol. 2, Program
Profiles). Washington, DC: Association for Community Based
Education.

Association for Community Based Education. (1989). *ACBE
evaluations of community based literacy programs 1988–89.*
Washington, DC: Association for Community Based Education.

Bandura, A. (1977). Self-efficacy: Toward a unifying theory of behavioral change. *Psychological Review, 37,* 191–215.

Barsch, J. (1981). The learning disabled adult: Self concept revisited.
Adult Literacy and Basic Education, 5, 172–179.

Beder, H. (1979). *The impact of adult education legislation on local
design and delivery: The case of the Adult Education Act.* Washington, DC: The National Institute of Education.

Beder, H. (1980). Reaching the hard to reach through effective marketing. In G. Darkenwald (Ed.), *Reaching the hard to reach in
continuing education* (pp. 11–26). San Francisco: Jossey-Bass.

163

Beder, H. (1986). The basic principles and concepts of marketing. In H. Beder (Ed.), *Marketing continuing education programs* (pp. 3–18). San Francisco: Jossey-Bass.

Beder, H. (1989a). *Reasons for nonparticipation among Iowa adults who are eligible for ABE.* Des Moines, IA: Iowa Department of Education.

Beder, H. (1989b). Purposes and philosophies of adult education. In S. B. Merriam & P. M. Cunningham (Eds.), *Handbook of adult and continuing education* (pp. 37–50). San Francisco: Jossey-Bass.

Beder, H. (1989c). Popular education in Latin America. In *Proceedings of the 30th annual adult education research conference* (pp. 25–30). Madison, WI: University of Wisconsin, Madison.

Beder, H. (1990a) Reasons for nonparticipation in adult basic education. *Adult Education Quarterly, 40,* 207–218.

Beder, H. (1990b). Reaching ABE students: Lessons from the Iowa studies. *Adult Literacy and Basic Education, 14,* 1–18.

Beder, H. W., & Darkenwald, G. (1974). *Development, demonstration and dissemination: Case studies of selected special projects in adult basic education.* Syracuse, NY: Syracuse Publications in Continuing Education.

Beder, H., & Quigley, B. A. (1990). Beyond the classroom. *Adult learning, 1,* (5), 19–21.

Beder, H., & Valentine, T. (1987). *Iowa's adult basic education students: Descriptive profiles based on motivations, cognitive ability, and sociodemographic variables.* Des Moines, IA: Iowa Department of Education.

Beder, H., & Valentine, T. (1990). Motivational profiles of adult basic education students. *Adult Education Quarterly, 40,* 78–94.

Bergevin, P. (1967). *A philosophy for adult education.* New York: Seabury Press.

Blais, J., Duquette, A., & Painchaud, G. (1989). Deterrents to womens' participation in work-related educational activities. *Adult Education Quarterly, 39,* 224–234.

Boggs, D. L., Buss, T. F., & Yarnell, S. M. (1979). Adult basic education in Ohio: A program impact evaluation. *Adult Education, 29,* 123–140.

Bordieu, P., & Passeron, J. C. (1977). *Reproduction in education, society and culture.* Beverly Hills, CA: Sage.

Bormouth, J. R. (1975). Reading literacy: Its definition and assessment. In J. B. Carroll & J. S. Chall (Eds.), *Toward a literate society.* New York: McGraw Hill.

Boshier, R. (1971). Motivational orientations of adult education participants: A factor analytic exploration of Houle's Typology. *Adult Education, 21,* 3–26.

Boshier, R. (1973). Educational participation and dropout: A theoretical model. *Adult Education, 23,* 255–282.

Boshier, R. (1976). Factor analysis at large: A critical review of the motivational orientation literature. *Adult Education, 27,* 24–47.

Boshier, R. (1977). Motivational orientations revisited: Life space motives and the educational participation scale. *Adult Education, 27,* 89–115.

Boshier, R. (1979). Effects of fees on clientele characteristics and participation in adult education. *Adult Education, 29,* 151–169.

Boshier, R., & Collins, J. B. (1985). The Houle Typology after twenty-two years: A large scale empirical test. *Adult Education Quarterly, 35,* 113–130.

Boucouvalas, M., & Krupp, J. (1989). Adult development and learning. In S. B. Merriam & P. M. Cunningham (Eds.), *Handbook of adult education* (pp. 183–200). San Francisco: Jossey-Bass.

Bova, B. M. (1985). Participation patterns of ABE students. *Adult Literacy and Basic Education, 9,* 95–105.

Burgess, P. (1971). Reasons for participation in group educational activities. *Adult education, 22,* 3–29.

California State Department of Education. (1989). *Adult education for the 21st century: Strategic plan to meet California's long-term adult education needs* (Summary Report). Sacramento, CA: Author.

Carp, A., Peterson, R., & Roelfs, P. (1975). Adult learning interests and experiences. In K. P. Cross & J. Valley (Eds.), *Planning nontraditional programs* (pp. 11–52). San Francisco: Jossey-Bass.

CASAS. (1990). Life skills competency list, June 1990. San Diego, CA: Comprehensive Adult Student Assessment System.

Center for Education Statistics. (1987). *Digest of education statistics 1987.* Washington, DC: Office of Research and Improvement, United States Department of Education.

Cervero, R. (1985). Is a common definition of literacy possible? *Adult Education Quarterly, 36,* 50–55.

Champagne, D., & Young, R. (1980). The self-concept of the adult basic education student. *Adult Literacy and Basic Education, 4*, 185–192.

Chisman, F. P. (1989). *Jump start: The federal role in adult literacy education.* Washington, DC: The Southport Institute.

Chisman, F. P. (1990). Solving the literacy problem in the 1990s: The leadership agenda. In F. Chisman & Associates (Eds.), *Leadership for literacy: The agenda for the 1990s* (pp. 246–264). San Francsico: Jossey-Bass.

Clark, A., & Hall, A. (1983). Self concepts and occupational aspirations levels of ABE students. *Adult Literacy and Basic Education, 6*, 4–6.

Clark, A., Smith, E., & Harvey, R. (1982). The self concepts and occupational aspirations of ABE & GED students. *Adult Literacy and Basic Education, 6*, 189–194.

Clearinghouse on Adult Education and Literacy. (1989). Adult literacy in the U.S.A.: A little or a lot (Report No. L-17). Washington, DC: Division of Adult Education and Literacy, United States Department of Education.

Close, G. R. W. (1981). An investigation of factors related to selected dimensions of the self-concept of ABE students. *Dissertation Abstracts International. 42*, 1900A.

Commission on Workforce Quality and Labor Market Efficiency. (1989). *Investing in people: A strategy to address America's workforce crisis.* Washington, DC: United States Department of Labor.

Cross, K. P. (1981). *Adults as learners: Increasing participation and facilitating learning.* San Francisco: Jossey-Bass.

Csikszentmihalyi, M. (1990). Literacy and intrinsic motivation. *Daedalus, 119* (2), 115–140.

Darkenwald, G. (1986). *Adult literacy education: A review of the research & priorities for future inquiry.* New York: Literacy Assistance Center, Inc.

Darkenwald, G. (1988). Comparison of deterrents to adult education participation in Britain and the United States. *Transatlantic dialogue: A research exchange: Proceedings of the SCUTREA/ AERC/CASAE conference* (pp. 126–131). Leeds, UK: University of Leeds.

Darkenwald G., & Merriam S. (1982). *Adult education: Foundations of practice.* New York: Harper and Row.

Darkenwald G., & Valentine, T. (1984). *Outcomes and impact of adult basic education.* New Brunswick, NJ: Center for Adult Development, Rutgers University, Graduate School of Education.

Darkenwald, G., & Valentine, T. (1985). Factor structure of deterrents to participation. *Adult Education Quarterly, 39,* 177–193.

Development Associates. (1980). *An assessment of the state-administered program of the Adult Education Act.* Arlington, VA: Author.

Division of Adult Education and Literacy. (1989). *Fact sheet: Adult education.* Washington, DC: Division of Adult Education and Literacy, Unites States Department of Education.

Ehringhaus, M. E. (1990). Media rhetoric and adult literacy. In T. Valentine (Ed.), *Beyond rhetoric: Fundamental issues in adult literacy education (Symposium Version)* (pp. 1–25). Athens, GA: University of Georgia, Department of Adult Education.

Elias, J. L., & Merriam, S. (1980). *Philosophical foundations of adult education.* Malabar, FL: Krieger.

Falk, C. F. (1986). Promoting continuing education programs. In H. Beder (Ed.), *Marketing continuing education* (pp. 49–72). San Francisco: Jossey-Bass.

Fingeret, A. (1983). Social networks: A new perspective on independence and illiterate adults. *Adult Education Quarterly, 33,* 133–146.

Fingeret, A. (1984). *Adult literacy education: Current and future directions.* Columbus, OH: ERIC Clearinghouse on Adult, Career and Vocational Education.

Fingeret, A. (1985). *North Carolina adult basic education evaluation 1985.* Raleigh, NC: North Carolina State University, Department of Adult and Community College Education.

Fingeret, A. (1989). The social and historical context of participatory literacy education. In A. Fingeret & P. Jurmo (Eds.), *Participatory literacy education* (pp. 5–15). San Francisco: Jossey-Bass.

Fingeret, A. (1990). Changing literacy instruction: Moving beyond the status quo. In F. Chisman & Associates (Eds.), *Leadership for literacy: The agenda for the 1990s* (pp. 25–50). San Francisco: Jossey-Bass.

Fingeret, A., & Jurmo, P. (Eds.). (1989). *Participatory literacy education.* San Francisco: Jossey-Bass.

Freire, P. (1970). *Pedagogy of the oppressed.* New York: Seabury.

Freire, P., & Macedo, D. (1987). *Literacy: Reading the word and the world.* South Hadley, MA: Bergin and Garvey.

Friedrich, O. (1990). Freed from greed? *Time Magazine.* January 1, 76–78.

Gans, H. (1962). *The urban villagers.* New York: The Free Press.

Garrison, D. R. (1985). Predicting dropout in adult basic education using interaction effects among school and nonschool variables. *Adult Education Quarterly, 36,* 25–38.

Giroux, H. A. (1983). *Theories and resistance in education: A pedagogy for the opposition.* South Hadley, MA: Bergin and Garvey.

Giroux, H. (1987). Literacy and the pedagogy of political empowerment. In P. Freire & D. Macedo (Eds.), *Literacy: Reading the word and the world* (pp. 1–27). South Hadley, MA: Bergin and Garvey.

Giroux, H., & Aronowitz, S. (1985). *Education under siege.* South Hadley, MA: Bergin and Garvey.

Goffman, E. G. (1974). *Stigma: Notes on the management of spoiled identity.* New York: Jason Aronson.

Gold, P. C., & Johnson, J. A. (1981). Entry level achievement characteristics of youth and adults reading below the fifth level: A preliminary profile and analysis. *Adult Literacy and Basic Education, 5,* 197–207.

Griffith, W. (1990). Beyond the mythical rhetoric. In T. Valentine (Ed.), *Beyond the rhetoric: Fundamental issues in adult literacy education (Symposium Version)* (pp. 53–79). Athens, GA: University of Georgia, Department of Adult Education.

Griffith, W., & Cervero, R. (1977). The adult performance level program: A serious and deliberate examination. *Adult Education, 27,* 209–224.

Hamilton, E., & Cunningham, P. M. (1990). Community-based education. In S. B. Merriam and P. M. Cunningham (Eds.), *Handbook of adult and continuing education* (pp. 439–450). San Francisco: Jossey-Bass.

Harris, L., & Associates. (1971). *The 1971 national reading difficulty index.* (ERIC Document Reproduction Service No. ED 057 312).

Hartwig, J. (1990). [Personal interview with John Hartwig, Iowa Department of Education, regarding the Iowa GED followup study]. Unpublished interview data.

Hayes, E. R. (1987). *Low-literate adult basic education students' perception of deterrents to participation.* Unpublished doctoral dissertation, Rutgers University, New Brunswick, NJ.

Hayes, E. R. (1988). A typology of low-literate adults based on perceptions of deterrents to participation in adult basic education. *Adult Education Quarterly, 39,* 1–10.

Heisel, M., & Larson, G. (1984). Literacy and social milieu: Reading behavior of the black elderly. *Adult Education Quarterly, 34,* 63–70.

Hill, S. T. (1987). *Trends in adult education 1969–1984.* Washington, DC: Center for Educational Statistics, United States Department of Education.

Hirsch, E. D. (1987). *Cultural literacy: What every American needs to know.* Boston: Houghton Mifflin.

Houle, C. O. (1961). *The inquiring mind.* Madison, WI: University of Wisconsin Press.

Huang, J., Benavot, A., & Cervero, R. (1990). *An analysis of structural factors associated with participation in state-funded adult basic education programs.* Paper presented at the annual meeting of the Adult Education Research Conference, Athens, GA.

Hunter, C. S., & Harman, D. (1979). *Adult literacy in the United States.* New York: McGraw-Hill.

Iowa Adult Literacy Studies Panel. (1989). [Policy issues raised by the Iowa Adult Literacy Studies]. Unpublished transcripts.

Irish, G. H. (1980). Reaching the least educated. In G. Darkenwald & G. Larson (Eds.), *Reaching hard-to reach adults* (pp. 39–54). San Francisco: Jossey-Bass.

✓James, M. (1990). Demystifying literacy: Reading, writing and the struggle for liberation. *Convergence, 23,* 14–25.

Johnston, W. B., & Packer, A. H. (1987). *Workforce 2000: Work and workers in the twenty-first century.* Indianapolis, IN: Hudson Institute.

Johnstone, J. W., & Rivera, R. J. (1965). *Volunteers for learning: A study of the educational pursuits of American adults.* Chicago: Aldine Publishing Company.

Jones, P. L., & Petry, J. P. (1980). *Evaluation of adult basic education in Tennessee.* Memphis, TN: Memphis State University, College of Education. (ERIC Documentation Reproduction Service No. ED 201 497).

Joseph, A. (1988). *The relationship between components of the ex-*

pectancy-valence model of motivation and participation of New Jersey public sector managers in job-related continuing education programs. Unpublished doctoral dissertation, Rutgers University, New Brunswick, NJ.

Jurmo, P. (1989). The case for participatory literacy education. In A. Fingeret & P. Jurmo (Eds.), *Participatory literacy education* (pp. 17–28). San Francisco: Jossey-Bass.

Kent, W. P. (1973). *A longitudinal evaluation of the adult basic education program.* Falls Church, VA: System Development Corporation.

Kerka, S. (1986). Deterrents to participation in adult education. *ERIC Digest, 59,* Columbus, OH: ERIC Clearinghouse on Adult, Career and Vocational Education.

Kidd, J. R. (1973). *How adults learn.* New York: Association Press.

Kirsch, I. S., & Junglebut, A. (1986). *Literacy: Profiles of America's young adults.* Princeton, NJ: Educational Testing Service.

Knowles, M. S. (1970). *The modern practice of adult education.* New York: Association Press.

Knowles, M. S. (1980). *The modern practice of adult education* (Rev. ed). Chicago: Follett.

Knox, A. B. (1977). *Adult development and learning: A handbook on individual growth and competence in the adult years for education and the helping professions.* San Francisco: Jossey-Bass.

Kotler, P. (1975). *Marketing for nonprofit organizations.* Englewood Cliffs, NJ: Prentice Hall.

Kozol, J. (1985). *Illiterate America.* Garden City, NY: Anchor Press.

Kreitlow, B. W., Glustrum, M., & Martin, C. (1981). *Educational needs assessment for Wisconsin adults with less than high school graduation or GED.* Madison, WI: Wisconsin State Board of Vocational, Technical and Adult Education.

Larson, G. A. (1980). Overcoming barriers to communications. In G. Darkenwald & G. Larson (Eds.), *Reaching hard-to-reach adults* (pp. 27–38). San Francisco: Jossey-Bass.

Lindeman, E. (1926). *The meaning of adult education.* New York: Republic.

Martin, L. G., & Fisher, J. C. (1990). Adult secondary education. In S. B. Merriam and P. M. Cunningham (Eds.), *Handbook of adult education* (pp. 478–490). San Francisco: Jossey-Bass.

Martindale, C. J., & Drake, J. B. (1989). Factor structure of deterrents to participation in off-duty adult education programs. *Adult Education Quarterly, 39,* 63–75.

Mason, R. C. (1986). Locating continuing education programs. In H. Beder (Ed.), *Marketing continuing education programs* (pp. 83–90). San Francisco: Jossey-Bass.

McClelland, S. (1972). *Project Reach final report, year 2.* South Bend, IN: Notre Dame University.

Mezirow, J., Darkenwald, G., & Knox, A. (1975). *Last gamble on education.* Washington, DC: Adult Education Association of the U.S.A.

Miller, H. L. (1967). *Participation of adults in education: A force-field analysis.* Boston: Center for the Study of Liberal Education for Adults.

Morstain, B. R., & Smart, S. C. (1974). Reasons for participation in adult education courses: A multivariate analysis of group differences. *Adult Education, 24,* 83–98.

Mortimer, J., & Simmons, R. G. (1978). Adult socialization. *Annual Review of Sociology, 4,* 421–454.

National Assessment of Educational Progress. (1976). *Adult work skills and knowledge.* Washington, DC: National Center for Educational Statistics.

NJALL, (1990). *Help wanted: A competent workforce for the 21st Century.* Glassboro, NJ: Author.

Office of Vocational and Adult Education. (1989). *State administered program—annual performance report* (Code DAE88D). Washington, DC: Division of Adult Education and Literacy, United States Department of Education.

Olds, E. B. (1952). *Financing adult education in America's public schools and community councils.* Washington, DC: Adult Education Association of the U.S.A.

Packer, A. H., & Campbell, W. L. (1990). Using computer technology for adult literacy education: Realizing the potential. In F. Chisman and Associates (Eds.), *Leadership for literacy: The agenda for the 1990s* (pp. 122–143). San Francisco: Jossey-Bass.

Porter, L. W., & Lawler, E. E. (1968). *Managerial attitudes and performance.* Chicago: Richard D. Irwin.

Program Services Branch. (1990). *Major federal programs supporting adult literacy efforts in U.S. Department of Education.* Washington, DC: Division of Adult Education and Literacy, United States Department of Education.

Pugsley, R. (1987). *National data update; Annual conference state directors of adult education.* Washington, DC: Division of Adult Education, United States Department of Education.

172   References

Pugsley, R. (1990). *Vital statistics: Who is served by the adult education program.* Washington, DC: Division of Adult Education and Literacy, United States Department of Education.

Quigley, B. A. (1989). *Reasons for resistance to ABE and recommendations for new delivery models and instructional strategies for the future.* Monroeville, PA: Continuing and Graduate Education Center, Pennsylvania State University.

Quigley, B. A. (1990a). *"This immense evil": The history of literacy education as social policy.* In T. Valentine (Ed.), *Beyond rhetoric: Fundamental issues in adult literacy education (Symposium Version)* (pp. 186–219). Athens, GA: University of Georgia, Department of Adult Education.

Quigley, B. A. (1990b). Hidden logic: Reproduction and resistance in adult literacy and basic education. *Adult Education Quarterly, 40,* 103–115.

Rachal, J. R. (1990). The social context of adult and continuing education. In S. B. Merriam & P. M. Cunningham (Eds.), *Handbook of adult education* (pp. 3–14). San Francisco: Jossey-Bass.

Rosenthal, N. (1990). Active learning/empowered learning. *Adult Learning, 1,* 16–18.

Rubenson, K. (1977). *Participation in recurrent education: A research review.* Paper presented at the meeting of the National Delegates on Developments in Recurrent Education, Paris, March, 1977.

Russ-Eft, D., & McLaughlin, D. H. (1981). *Technical report 22: Analysis of issues in adult basic education.* Palo Alto, CA: Statistical Analysis Group in Education, American Institute for Research.

Scanlan, C. L. (1986). *Deterrents to participation: An adult education dilemma.* Columbus, OH: ERIC Clearinghouse on Adult, Career, and Vocational Education.

Scanlan, C. L., & Darkenwald, G. (1984). Identifying deterrents to participation in continuing education. *Adult Education Quarterly, 34,* 155–166.

Scribner, S. (1984). Literacy in three metaphors. *American Journal of Education, 91,* 6–21.

Scribner, S., & Cole, M. (1981). *The psychology of literacy.* Cambridge, MA: The Harvard University Press.

Sloan, J. W. (1984). *Public policy in Latin America: A comparative survey.* Pittsburgh, PA: University of Pittsburgh Press.

Stack, C. B. (1974). *All our kin.* New York: Harper and Row.

Stein, S. (1990). Workplace literacy as a model for good literacy practice. In T. Valentine (Ed.), *Beyond rhetoric: Fundamental issues in adult literacy education (Symposium Version)* (pp. 279–318). Athens, GA: University of Georgia, Department of Adult Education.

Sticht, T. G., & Mikulecky, L. (1984). *Job-related basic skills: Cases and conclusions.* Columbus, OH: ERIC Clearinghouse on Adult, Career and Vocational education.

Taylor, M. C. (1990). Adult basic education. In S. B. Merriam and P. M. Cunningham (Eds.), *Handbook of adult education* (pp. 465–477). San Francisco: Jossey-Bass.

Tough, A. M. (1982). *Intentional changes: A fresh approach to helping people change.* New York: Cambridge University Press.

United States Department of Education. (1989). State administered adult education programs and secretary's discretionary programs for adult education; final regulations. *Federal Register, 54* (159), August 18, 1989, Washington, DC: United States Department of Education.

Usher, R., & Bryant, I. (1987). *Adult education as theory, practice, and research: The captive triangle.* London: Routledge.

Valentine, T. (1986a). Adult functional literacy as a goal of instruction. *Adult Education Quarterly, 36* 108–113.

Valentine, T. (1986b). *Issues central to the definition of adult functional literacy.* Washington, DC: Office of Higher Education and Adult Learning, United States Department of Education.

Valentine, T. (1990). What motivates adults to participate in the federal adult basic education program? *Research on Adult Basic Education, 1,* 1–2.

Valentine, T., & Darkenwald, G. (1986). The benefits of GED graduation and a typology of graduates. *Adult Education Quarterly, 37,* 23–35.

Van Tilberg, E., & DuBois, J. (1989). *Literacy students' perceptions of successful participation in adult education: A cross-cultural approach through expectancy valence.* Paper presented at the 30th Annual Adult Education Research Conference, University of Wisconsin, Madison, April 27–29.

Vroom, V. H. (1964). *Work and motivation.* New York: John Wiley and Sons.

Walker, S. M., Ewert, D. M., & Whaples, G. (1981). *Perceptions of program impact in Maryland.* College Park, MD: University of Maryland. (ERIC Document Reproduction Service No. ED 107–201).

Weber, R. M. (1977). Adult literacy in the United States. In T. P. Gorman (Ed.), *Language and literacy: Current research and issues.* Teheran, Iran: International Institute for Adult Literacy Methods. (ERIC Document Reproduction Service No. ED 179 923).

Willard, J. C., & Warren, L. A. (1986). Developing program offerings. In H. Beder (Ed.), *Marketing continuing education programs* (pp. 29–48). San Francisco: Jossey-Bass.

Willis, P. E. (1978). *Learning to labour.* Guildford, Surrey, UK: Biddles, Ltd.

Wilson, R. C. (1980). Personological variables related to GED retention and withdrawal. *Adult Education, 30,* 173–185.

AUTHOR INDEX

SUBJECT INDEX